We were fortunate
indeed, to have the
great priviledge of
being kids in those
good old days, and
in this book we can
recall & relive, in our
memories, some of the
wonderful experiences
of our childhood.
  I thank God for the
joy of growing up in those
days with our wonderful
family.   Don

YOU AND I AND YESTERDAY

You and I and Yesterday

by Marjorie Holmes

William Morrow & Company, Inc.   NEW YORK   1973

ILLUSTRATIONS BY BOB BRUNSON

Copyright © 1973 by Marjorie Holmes

Grateful acknowledgment is made to *Today's Health*, pub-
lished by the American Medical Association, for permission
to reprint "Motoring Marvels of Yesteryear," "We Made
Our Own Music," "Winter Is My 'Memory Season,'" "All
Doors Led to the Kitchen," "Days of Movie Magic,"
"Every Child Was King—in a Swing," "Golden Days in
Grandpa's Garden," "Give Me an Old-Fashioned Peddler,"
"What Does an Apron Mean?" "Whatever Happened to
Run, Sheep, Run," and "Mother's Wonderful Wishing-
Book," copyright © 1966, 1967, 1968, 1970 by American
Medical Association; and to Doubleday & Company, Inc.,
for permission to reprint "Mother's Wonderful Wishing
Book," copyright © 1966 by American Medical Associa-
tion, "Mother's Apron," copyright © 1967 by American
Medical Association, which originally appeared in *Today's
Health*, published by the American Medical Association,
from the book *Love and Laughter*, by Marjorie Holmes.

Printed in the United States of America.

Library of Congress Catalog Card Number 73-7386

ISBN 0-688-00153-X

2   3   4   5   76   75   74   73

For Harold, Gwen and Barney

CONTENTS

INTRODUCTION

Why are we looking backward? Why do we find so much joy and solace in the past?

Time and distance always lend enchantment. Those of us who remember the Good Old Days can be expected to view them through the rosy spectacles of nostalgia. What is surprising is that so many of this generation seem to be sharing that view! Is it because they don't like Today and are scared of Tomorrow? . . . They are trying to find Yesterday. The yesterday of their parents and even their grandparents. The exact era doesn't matter, just so it's the past.

They have raided the trunks in our attics and consulted our picture albums to assume its disguise: in bell-bottoms and beards and sideburns; in granny dresses that sweep the streets or miniskirts that mimic the Flapper; in beaded headbands that *my* generation thought quaint. . . . In a dozen ways they are trying to identify with it, adopt it for themselves.

They are reviving the Oldies but Goodies in songs and records and movies. They are patronizing, and running, restaurants that resemble my grandmother's Victorian parlor, or my mother's dining room—complete with golden oak buffet and china cabinet and Maxfield Parrish pictures on the wall. On a cross-country trip last summer I came across these anachronisms everywhere; not antique-filled artsy-craftsy places catering to the tearoom set—no, they were youth hangouts serving beer and hamburgers and Reuben sandwiches and ice-cream sodas. And, as with so many things that we first protest in our progeny and then take over, these places were also lively with their elders, many of *them* bearded and beaded or otherwise costumed as if for a trip into Yesterday!

Young people (and others too) are even going back to the Old Time Religion.

A few years ago there was a lot of screaming about "God is dead!" And in many ways He was. Drained of life and meaning in many churches, battered and crucified and buried by the very society that claimed "In God we trust." Buried under its social injustices, its materialism and cynicism. But you can't bury anything so potent as God without life bursting forth stronger than ever. A rich and fruitful harvest has sprung up, and its seeds are spreading beyond anyone's wildest dreams. Vast numbers have joined the Jesus movement. They are flocking to revivals and old-fashioned Camp Meetings. They are filling the charismatic churches where the Holy Spirit is manifested in healing and speaking in tongues.

Young people are witnessing in the streets, touring the country in caravans, living in Christian communes with rules more strict than any parents would have dared impose. It's as if the excesses to which this generation has been subjected—violence and drugs and sexual license, the breakdown of law and order—have driven many of them to an opposite spiritual extreme. They are bypassing their parents (whether those parents faithfully went to conventional churches every Sunday, or spent the day downing drinks at the country club), proclaiming a "new religion," which is actually the old impassioned fervor of the early church. And while this may shock and dismay a lot of people, I see it as a part of the head-on collision we are facing between good and evil. I say, "Praise the Lord!"

But back to the Good Old Days. Were they all that good? No, frankly not. Certainly not that Bonnie-and-Clyde era, the Depression; I would not want to go through that again. The pain and humiliation of that desperate time left scars. But the Depression stiffened our backs and toughened our moral muscles. Nobody brainwashed us into thinking that the government owed us a living. Instead, our own survival instinct made us realize that *we owed life* something. Our best efforts, our best fight. The scars the Depression dealt us were honorable scars.

The "good" in the Good Old Days seems to me that there was more love than hate, more kindness than cruelty, more decency than dirt, more peace than violence, and where I lived almost no crime. There were a few scandals, yes, but the fact that they were considered "scandals" emphasized the rarity of the breaking of the moral codes. There were a few town drunks but alcoholism was almost unknown; nice people simply didn't drink, at least not where I lived, not during Prohibition. "Gay" meant a grand time was had at a church sociable or somebody's house. Our knowledge of drug addiction was limited to one or two grim movies about tragic derelicts known as "dope fiends."

It was a time of being safe, being sheltered, being loved. Not of being satisfied, no, but of looking excitedly toward the future. A time when the American dream still beckoned, when everything hadn't been invented yet, everything hadn't been experienced. When there was some mystery, some sense of adventure, of romance—and yes, some reason for being ambitious, wanting to "get some-place."

The pieces that follow are memories of that time, compared with the world as my children have found it. I started my family early and had my last child late, with almost a generation gap separating the ones in between. (Our oldest graduated from college the year the youngest started kindergarten.) This has given me almost a forty-year span of parenthood in which to match my Yesterdays against the Todays that will someday be *my* children's past.

And who knows? Maybe through the rosy spectacles of nostalgia they will find their own Yesterdays sweet!

I hope so.

I

The Kites and Rites of Spring

Spring is a miracle wherever it happens. Buds break, robins return, and softly, softly, stealing over the land, comes the hazing green. Like smoke unsure of its destination, it seems to hover above the trees. Then the green settles, clings, the air is golden, children beg to go wrapless to school, and everywhere is heard the perennial sounds of children in league with spring: the slap of jumping ropes, the chuckle of jacks on a flat stone step, the whirring hum of roller skates. While overhead, as if testing the sky, the kites soar.

Such things are eternal.

But who can really appreciate spring who has not spent a hard snow-shackled winter in a little town? They say the winters are changing, they don't have it so hard anymore, but when I was small in Storm Lake, Iowa, snow began to fall around Thanksgiving, and it was months before we ever saw the ground. It fell and blew and drifted and fell again; blizzards stopped the trains. Sometimes people got lost in the blizzards and froze to death. Farm women helped deliver each other's babies when the doctors couldn't get through. Cars and fences were buried, and you could often walk atop the white castles of the drifts. Winter was a drama fraught with possible death— and delight. Skating on the lake. And the huge buffalo fish that could be speared, Eskimo fashion, by squatting beside the air holes in the ice. The hayrides, snuggled down in a bobsled with a harsh smelly blanket and a boy . . . The time the basketball team and half the town were stranded in Des Moines and had to sleep in the gym and had a high old time.

But after a while you got sick of the whole business. The eternal shoveling and wading and having to bundle up every time you went outdoors. The bitter sting of frost-bite in spite of mittens and overshoes and scarves. The snow that got dirty and yellow, and ice that meant you could slip and fall and break a leg. "Won't spring ever come?" you began to despair.

Then it happened, or seemed to. The sun began to beam, the fierce white locks of winter to yield, to lose their grip. Icicles made a dripping music from the eaves, the trees stretched, shook off their white fur coats. You could hear their branches crackling in the night, like people who've let their bones go to sleep. Snowbanks softened and sank, gutters ran foaming streams. And on the sidewalks, walking to school, appeared beautiful ponds that mirrored the trees and your own elated face. Looking down . . . down . . . was like joining the princesses who ran away and danced their slippers to ribbons in a mysterious land beneath a magical lake.

The air was suddenly unbearably soft and sweet. You leaped the puddles or splashed recklessly through them, you ran and shouted, gone a little mad with spring. . . .

Then came the rude awakening. Literally, in the morning, you awoke to snow again! Having teased you, roused your hopes, winter was back. In helpless indignation you watched it settling in. How dared it! You had seen a robin, picked a pussy willow. And often, as if to taunt you, this last return engagement was even more grim.

Now there was all that melting to be gone through again. You didn't quite trust it the second time, fearful of false hopes. But the sun's smile was insistent, reassuring, and the grass was undeniably coming up—surely it knew what it was doing. The sidewalks were lively with lavender worms and riddled with budscales and little winged seedpods that popped when you stepped on them.

It was time to get out your jacks or buy a little jingling bag of new ones. Time to check your skates and the size of your ball of string. Nobody had yet thought of simply sticking merchandise into a paper sack; everything you bought was wrapped in a length of paper ripped from a giant roll in the store and tied with string. And everybody saved string. An old man out near Newell was said to have achieved a roll weighing one hundred pounds. Some women of obsessive thrift and patience crocheted string into potholders and doilies, even rugs. Kids saved string for one purpose, for flying kites.

My brother, who had a paper route, could extravagantly buy his kite cord. The rest of us were content with our knotty but ever-fattening globes. Paper was saved, too. Mother would iron it for us, testing the flatiron first with a moist, sizzling finger. The paper crackled and a pleasant scorchy smell mingled with that of our flour-and-water paste. Huddled around the kitchen table, we made our kites, crossing thin pieces of wooden lathe and carefully fitting the paper around their frames. Fragile paper birds, diamond shaped, with gay tails of ribbon and colored scraps.

"Don't get it too heavy or it won't fly," we were warned.

I always knew, with a kind of sorrowing desperation, that my kite wouldn't fly anyway, no matter what. At least *I* couldn't make it fly. However bright the day or brisk the wind, my kite humiliatingly dragged behind my heels like an exasperating child. Sometimes it strove feebly, rose a little, like my hopes, then flopped about like a wounded thing. Nobody else had this problem. Up and up their kites staggered, nosing their way as if to discover the best route to the sky. There they soared, as confident as the gulls above the lake, tugging at the fingers that held their frail leash.

Harold could fly a kite, Gwen could fly a kite, even our little brother Barney could fly a kite, aided by our father. *Mother* could fly a kite, dashing along the shore with her skirts blowing back against her legs, her white teeth flashing. Babe, the gay little gypsy who practically lived with us after her mother died, could fly a kite as skillfully as any boy. Yet I could only stand humiliated and awed, watching the lovely antics of theirs dipping and gliding with such mystery and freedom up where we could not follow.

The others tried to show me, help me, or do it for me; and when they had gotten my kite off the ground I could feel its wild heart pulsing down the string. But it wasn't the same as putting it into the sky myself, and one of the sad defeats of my childhood was that I never learned.

Farther and farther Harold would let his string out

until his ship was but a speck in space. Sometimes it got away, hesitating, turning back as if to look over its shoulder for a final glimpse, struggling, not sure it wanted to leave. A wistful sense of loss and excitement would send us chasing off in the direction it was heading for a little way. Where was it going? To have fashioned something that could rise so high, travel so far before it fell—where? The bodies of runaway kites were often to be seen forlornly clutched in trees nearby—who knew where they came from? Another county maybe, another state—even from China or some other land across the sea!

Like robins and kites and pussy willows, spring meant roller skates. Once the walks were clear we would go plowing through boot-clogged closets to dig them out. Often they didn't fit and the frantic cry would go up, "I've got to have new skates!" And, oh, the thrill of those new ones (especially after lots of battered hand-me-downs); their nuggety weight in the box, the smell of their shiny leather, and the smooth purring music they made when the wheels were slapped.

I feel sorry for children living in sidewalkless suburbia if only because it means there's no place to skate. True, it means no skates lying around to stumble over, no wheels to be oiled, clamps to be tightened, skate keys to be lost. But something else is surely lost if a child's portion of the world is not generously ribboned with sidewalks to be discovered, explored, commanded in soaring splendor on skates.

Sidewalks have personalities, a little bit like the people who traverse them, in a little town. We were on intimate terms with all those in our neighborhood, and beyond. The ones so bumpy they made our teeth rattle as we skimmed along. The broken-down ones with cracked old faces. We learned to jump the cracks; otherwise we had to stop and go clopping along beside them on the grass. We knew the stretches smooth as satin where our wheels crooned as we gathered speed and the cross-cracks made a rhythmic clicking like a train.

We skated near home and we skated the broad, lovely walks of the parks. Sometimes we skated clear downtown, rolling into the frosty air of Mike Tracy's, over to the counter where we sat spooning sundaes, our feet dangling heavy as the hooves of farm workhorses. Mike was always scolding because he said we'd ruin his floor, but he never stinted on the ice cream. We repeatedly skated the block around the Presbyterian Church, mainly because the church had an ever-bubbling fountain to quench our skating thirst.

Above it were engraved the words: "And whosoever shall give a cup of cold water to one of these little ones . . ." We didn't feel little; in fact we felt so big we owned that fountain just as we owned the sidewalks and the town.

No special day escaped our celebration, even April Fool's Day. We lay awake nights trying to think up tricks to play on people, and settled for the old ones: salt in sugar bowls, catsup in the syrup pitcher, a pocketbook on the walk to be snatched away with a string. We made up a batch of fudge and poured it over cotton balls before it hardened, to be offered to the unsuspecting the next day.

But April was primarily preparation for May. During April we worked on our May baskets with our hoarded supplies of ribbons and paper lace and boxes. Shoe boxes and cookie boxes and the boxes the big wooden matches came in; and candy boxes, those treasures already so pretty it was almost a shame to cover them up. Night after night we labored, with scissors and more little jar lids of paste, ruffling the dry crinkly crepe paper, rolling the tissue-paper flowers. Shelves and dressers became harbor for this fleet of lovely craft, and we would stand before it in a torment of admiration, trying to decide which was the most beautiful and on whom to bestow it.

On the first of May we dashed home from school to start making candy and popping corn. Mother would have already made a batch or two and at least one dishpanful of popcorn. "When I was a girl we filled our baskets with bouquets," she would remark. We thought this rather quaint and very dull—imagine not being able to eat the contents.

We were usually just finishing supper when the first thrilling rap on the porch would come, and we'd all hurl down our napkins to rush out to see who it was meant for, and try to catch the person who'd brought it. Then everything became a wild flurry as we tried to finish our own and steal off with them through the dusk. Sometimes handles broke and we had to come storming back to mend and refill. By then other baskets would have appeared, and the joy of finding them was appeasement. By the time the stars were out and parents were urgently calling, those that had arrived usually equaled the number you had delivered. Though sometimes, to your dismay, you got a gorgeous basket richly stuffed, from somebody you hadn't even remembered. Or, thrillingly minus a name— which could only mean, or at least you hoped, from a boy who loved you madly.

Anyway, we stuffed ourselves on the plunder the way kids do now after Trick or Treat on Halloween; and for weeks the pretty baskets adorned our rooms until, like the kites, they collapsed and were carried out with the trash.

Each year nearly every school had its official May Day rites. A maypole was erected on the lawn and gym classes did folk dances around it. The older girls got to do the maypole winding, an intricate process of prancing back and forth and ducking in and out in such a fashion that you braided a pattern of its pastel streamers.

I almost became a seventh-grade dropout, so great was my dread of this living puzzle and my approaching turn. "Don't worry, it's not hard, you can do it," people encouraged. I knew better. Some deep, dark knowledge warned me, much as it had informed me I'd never fly a kite.

Practicing was sheer torment. The grass was green, birds sang, the sound of Miss Schultz's piano plinking away where it had been hauled out into the sunshine was lively, the scent of nearby appleblossoms was sweet. The colored streamers blew from the maypole enticingly. Other girls in bloomers and middy blouses gamboled about without a care, but my heavy heart was in my feet. "Just take your pink one and circle the green, then back between the blue and the white—here, I'll show you." Miss Winters walked with me, patiently, in and out, ducking the blithe spirits dipping all about us. I was okay as long as she held on, but the minute she let go I panicked.

"To the right, now *under*, now to the left, now *back* . . ." I bumped into Aleda Womack, soaring lightly toward me; nearly knocked down Ruth Rydstrom. Even Ruth, all corkscrew curls and with the grace of a boxcar, could do it—she had a logical, mathematical mind. Despairing, Miss Winters finally summoned my younger sister to take my place. I was relieved but very ashamed. Worse, the dancers got to wear Grecian tunics made out of white sheets, and crisscross ribbons up their legs. I didn't mourn the tunics so much, but I had always wanted to wear those crisscross ribbons.

Then at the last minute my sister came down with the mumps. Miss Winters didn't have much choice—it was either use me or call off the whole thing. She decided to risk it. I had no choice either—I'd already *had* the mumps. And maybe it was those crisscross Grecian laces, maybe the fact that Tom McCreery was watching, maybe it was the sheer singing beauty of the day—but I leaped about as nimbly as Aleda, pranced with the precision of Ruth, and finished the reel with only one slight hitch. By that time the glee club was singing "Waterlilies," and they were getting ready to crown the queen. I couldn't have been any happier if they had put the wreath of roses on my brow.

Spring officially ended with Memorial or Decoration Day. To commemorate the dead of the Civil War, Mother explained, and honor not only its dead but our own. For years while the G.A.R. (Grand Army of the Republic) was active, there was always a parade. The band played, the "Old Soldiers," as we called them, marched or rode in cars, followed by the veterans of the First World War. Then came various dignitaries, and high school girls carrying flowers, and finally a float trimmed with red, white, and blue bunting and bearing a real live Uncle Sam.

We crouched on the curbs of Main Street bursting with pride. Uncle Sam was always Grandpa Holmes, who had a big nose and a jutting white goatee and was born to the part. Tall and erect in his costume, he would bow grandly and doff his hat to people, passing by. We were in awe of him even without the trappings and to see him thus was to be almost overwhelmed. We waved timidly, hoping he'd notice and wink or grin or give us a special nod, but I don't recall that he ever did. He had sired thirteen children and he didn't care much for kids now.

Grandpa Griffith was usually the one who took us to the parade and later to the services in Chautauqua Park. The big echoing pavilion rang to patriotic oratory; then everybody would trek down across the grass to the docks where the girls, in their white dresses, would be handed daintily into boats and rowed out onto the lake. The flag was lowered to half-mast. And while the band played "The Battle Hymn of the Republic" and "We're Tenting Tonight on the Old Camp Ground," the girls strewed their flowers on the water. Then "America," while the Old Soldiers, in wheelchairs some of them, or leaning on their canes, threw back their shoulders and saluted as best they could, while the tears rolled down their cheeks.

Walking home, Grandpa Griffith would tell us tales of the Civil War. He'd been too young to go, but his brother had. Toward the end, fearful it was going to be over before he got there, he ran away and joined up, but his sister and brother-in-law went after him and dragged him home. "And threshed me good."

We pressed closer to his side, and nuzzled his callused hand. The thought of anybody's ever hitting Grandpa even as a boy was almost too awful to believe.

The ranks of Old Soldiers thinned every year and after a while there was only one of them left, old Mr. Matson. After a while, too, even Grandpa Griffith was gone and so was Uncle Sam. The band still played in the park and there were speeches and taps, but no more parades. But the day was busy anyway with getting flowers ready to carry to the cemeteries. Armloads of fat fragrant peonies from the bushes in the yard. Snowballs, shedding petals; delicately dancing bleeding hearts. Purple and yellow iris, which we called "flags." Sweet peas, lilies of the valley. Women ran back and forth across lawns sharing their flowers, offering, borrowing. And sometimes as if all this weren't enough, Dad bought roses and carnations at the greenhouse.

Every possible fruit jar and vase had been assembled and washed the night before, and now must be filled with water, since the faucets at the cemetery were always so busy. We all drove off at last, the Ford a jostling, slopping chariot bursting with people and flowers. The day was always hot and the fragrance almost overpowering. Mother would fan herself and mop her face with a white hand-kerchief trimmed with tatting.

We drove first to Alta where most of Mother's people were buried, and when the vases had been set tipsily on the green mounds, we would wander about reading the headstones, Mother giving a little roll call of relatives. "There's my baby sister Amy. . . . There's Uncle Foster, my favorite uncle, did you know he used to hide slaves for the underground? Of course that was long before I knew him. . . . There's Grandpa and Grandma Mills. . . ." After that we drove back to the lake and through the stone pillars that guarded the cemetery across from the Country Club. Here, in the crypts of a fine mausoleum built by Uncle Frank, rested together in peace at last (or so we hoped) Dad's numerous, often quarreling clan. Other important people of the town reposed here too, for Uncle Frank was something of an operator and he had sold them space. On the little shelves provided for the purpose the jars and vases of bright flowers were set, making the whole

place cheerful as a bridal chapel, especially with the sunshine streaming through the stained-glass window and
spinning rainbows on the floor.

When all these pilgrimages were finally accomplished,
we shed duty, decorum—and our clothes. At least the three
girls: Gwen, me, and Babe. Squirming into swimming suits
and snatching up towels, we streaked for the lake. Mother
usually calling plaintive futile remonstrances. "No, no,
please, it's too early, it's too cold, you'll catch pneumonia!"

But now that we were teens we had things to prove.
That we were bold and brave and independent and de-
serving of notice, even if it meant suffering the shock of
icy waters in order to be first in the lake. Other kids
watched with grudging admiration; Curt Bethards, who ran
the boathouse, called us damn fools but gave us each a
candy bar in tribute when we came out, blue and shaking.
Sometimes people took our pictures.

We had made a pact. In this manner we would mark
Memorial Day every year, and we did. It was our proud
personal baptism, our final rite of spring.

II

Golden Days
in Grandpa's Garden

The other day I saw a cartoon in which a little girl was tugging at her mother's sleeve in the market, exclaiming: "Look, Mommy, look—vegetables you don't even have to defrost!"

I laughed, but it also gave me a pang. I grieve for the children who grow up missing gardens; the thrill of spying that first pinstripe of green that signals the seeds are up in spring. The glory of lugging their own pumpkins in from among the cornstalks for Halloween. And, oh, the long luxurient feasts for both body and spirit that lie in the summer between!

Almost nobody raises gardens anymore, even in my small Iowa hometown. There, too, I find on nostalgic visits, land is at a premium and parents just as busy as they are in suburbia. Patios have replaced the potato patch, the grape arbor is now the two-car garage, and supermarkets boom where the old orchard used to be. Here and there, like some wistful monument to the past, an iron pump still stands. But its slender arm that you used to yank so vigorously to wash the garden stuff is rusted fast.

Its voice that used to creak and chortle as it gushed forth cold bright water over bare feet—or a turnip—is still. Vines claim it now, or a decorative housewife has enshrined its feet with petunias.

When I was growing up the garden was as much a part of the child's world as his mother's apron. Most of our food came straight from the garden. Also, the family garden was a kind of character symbol. The bigger and neater it was, the more worthy of respect. To have a little, scrabbly, half-hearted garden or a big unkempt one was to be labeled shiftless. And not to have a garden at all—well! You were either so impressively rich you could afford to buy from others, or so downright lazy you were probably on relief.

It was impossible to hide the state of your garden. People walked more then and, strolling past, cast frankly appraising eyes. Also, your garden flowed right up to the alley which bisected every block. If you hadn't weeded clear back to that cindery avenue the iceman might notice, or Judge Bailey taking his shortcut home.

Gardeners, whatever their era or locale, are of the earth earthy. They garden out of love. Such was my Grandpa Griffith. His garden was his passion and his pride. Although his garden was smaller after Grandma died, it was always as neat as a Grant Wood painting, its products blue-ribbon winners at the county fair. To him it was vital that vegetables be sown on Good Friday, and potatoes be planted dark of the moon. "When the moon comes out they sprout," he solemnly averred. Although we tended to spurn this as superstition we did so at our own risk. His potatoes *did* get to the table first, and always grew big and firm. Likewise, his radishes, green onions, and

lettuce generally outdistanced all rivals. And certainly surpassed ours.

For Mother, alas, did not inherit his earthy fervors
(she'd rather read), and Dad, a traveling salesman, didn't
either. It was generally Grandpa who saved the family
honor by lining up that prima donna of plowmen, Nate
Mitchell, and his horse, Daisy, to plow up our backyard.
It was Grandpa who lovingly polished rakes and spades
and sharpened hoes and scythes *screeee!* on his gritty
white grinding wheel. Grandpa, with his quality of gentle
urgency and enthusiasm, who worked us all into a lather
of vowing that *this* year we would have a really splendid
garden.

The arrival of Mr. Mitchell and Daisy was akin to
having aristocratic Miss Planalp condescend to take a
dumb, unpromising kid for music lessons. Thrilling but
awesome. It wasn't what Mr. Mitchell said, it was the
masterful way he strode the premises, kicking at last year's
stumps of cabbage, and shooting tobacco juice toward the
dry, sere remnants of cornstalks, bowed as if in supplica-
tion. And you knew as he bellowed "Gee-yaaap!" or
"H'yaaar!" and Daisy began her jingling journey that her
coppery nuggets had fertilized some of the best gardens
in town. They were all that was needed; for the soil that
began to roll and billow so magically from beneath his
great silver blades, was pitch black. We darted behind,
stamping its chocolaty richness under our feet, crumbling
its clods in our hands (or throwing them at each other).
They were mealy and moist and fragrant as only rich soil
can be. And from them poked the wary pink heads of
worms, which the boys would snatch and drop into tin
cans or chase the girls with, while blackbirds greedily
watched and scolded in rusty voices from the apple tree.

When the entire back lot had been transformed into
a black and stormy sea, Mr. Mitchell would attach a rake
to Daisy and comb and shape it all out into smoothly un-
dulating parallels, pleasantly satisfying as corduroy. Then
Grandpa would reward our private Piers Plowman from a
big snap purse (*"Thus they geven here golde, glotones to
kepe . . ."*). And when we'd all had a turn at petting Daisy
(the velvety prickle of her nose, her sweaty, sour-sweet
flanks, still shaggy with their winter coat), the real business of gardening would begin.

Dad always managed to be home for this event. Plotting and conferring as to where to put what, he and
Mother would drive the stakes and stretch the cords,
chalk-white against the black, so that the rows would be
straight. Meanwhile, all of us clamoring, "What can I do?
Let me help! Where's my garden? I want this corner. . . .
No, that's mine, Mama promised me!"

They were remarkably patient with us. Dad, balding
young, and chewing gum in his chipper way, would be both
funny and tender as he adjudicated claims, guided wobbly
hoes, and squatted to help eager fingers shake seeds into
trenches and cover them carefully.

Then after days of anxious watching the miracle occurred. You rushed out one morning to discover a few
beady trails of green. "The garden's up! Look, look." First,
the round pushy radish leaves; then the tiny points of
onions, and a delicate dance of lettuce sifting through.
Astoundingly soon your mother was sending you out to
see if any of this was big enough. And lo, probing among
the radishes' prickly leaves, testing the spindly threads
below, you uprooted a few rosy imp-faces with saucy tails.
Among the delicate spears of the onions were a few pearly
tips. And the lettuce was thick enough to cut, though the

leaves were still so delicate and small they clung babylike to your fingers, especially when you washed them in a big dishpan under the pump.

Mother always greeted this virgin offering with childish elation. "Oh, I could make a *meal* out of fresh garden stuff!" she would cry, heaping the bowls and lavishing her own with vinegar, salt, and pepper. So could we all. For with a glass of milk and plenty of bread and butter, who could ask for more? And these were only teasers for the succulent harvest to come.

But each day we were learning a lesson that no child of the supermarket can appreciate: that Nature, for all her bounty, gives you nothing scot-free. Soon we were being ordered forth with hoes merely to keep the weeds at bay. Or to chase off the rabbits, merry little hide-and-seek enemies that you couldn't hate even when they neatly sheared off an entire row of your very best broccoli. And though we fretted and fussed about aching backs and blisters, and ran in to look at the clock tocking away on the kitchen table, and begged to join the friends who'd managed their own release—the garden was a hot, humming, secretive, pungently sweet, and tantalizing place. With all its many products somehow like little people manifesting their different personalities.

The peas had an air of precious superiority. Their tendrils wound gracefully up the props and clung with delicate fingers; their blossoms were like tiny white bows in their hair. Then the green pods formed, at first limp and flat as a girl's bosom, but swelling, ripening against the day when you would descend, banging upon a pan. So few were they at first that you cheated, picking some that were barely formed. But peas develop fast. Soon their abundance made their gathering urgent. "Hurry, go pick the peas, or they'll be too old."

The pods became long and fat, so full some were bursting. No need to steal the flat ones, or those whose tough yellowing hides informed you you were already too late. Like people who have too swiftly reached their prime, they had had their chance, poor things.

The vessels overflowed. Sitting on sunny back steps, you shelled them. Birds sang, mothers worked in kitchens, screen doors banged. There was the crisp snapping of the pods. With a sensation vaguely sensuous, your fingers rooted out the emeralds they contained. Some you ate raw —juicy, flat, and faintly sweet. The shells piled up on a newspaper, like the wreckage of mighty fleets. You saved a few for little boats and sailed them later across a puddle or a big tin tub.

Potatoes were a lustier vegetable, but when they were babies they were creamed with peas to form a dish that would make the gods throw away their ambrosia and abandon Parnassus for our backyard.

Potato vines (like tomatoes) have starry blossoms, and potatoes are fun to dig. Grandpa always used a pitchfork, since the blade of spade or hoe was likely to slice them in two. I can see him yet, tall and handsome and white-moustached, the clods raining softly through his lifted tines, a few potatoes clinging to the parent root like small brown gnomes. The rest were buried treasure scattered about, and you hunted them with almost the same anticipation as you hunted eggs. These first little new potatoes had skin so fragile it could be scrubbed off with a stiff brush. The flesh underneath was rosy, exactly like that of children whose mother has washed their faces too hard.

Beans were pleasant to pick. They hung like lumpy pendants in the bushy forests of their growth, slender green string beans or the yellow wax ones that had a tallowy luster like their name. Surrounded by cohorts you were set to snapping and "stringing" them for the pot, already fragrant with ham or bacon, bubbling on the range. There is nothing more delicious than fresh-cooked beans, and time only enhances their flavor when they're cold. Often, snooping in the icebox at bedtime, there would be a squabble over who got to scoop aside the grease and finish off a bowl.

Sweet corn was royal fare. It grew tall and stately out by the alley, hobnobbing with the hollyhocks and sunflowers. On hot nights you could sometimes hear it crackling as it stretched its joints toward the stars, like the field corn on nearby farms. We watched its development with hungry eyes, measuring our own growth against it, standing on tiptoe sometimes to pull aside the rosy silks and test the kernels with a fingernail. When the ears were ready they spurted milk, and off you streaked with the news. In a blissful suspense you waited while Father or Grandfather came to check; and what joy when he broke the ear free, stripped the husks aside and waved the nude ear aloft like some triumphant offering. "Sweet corn for supper!" The word spread. And we came squealing like pigs to the trough and ate it from the steaming golden platters with butter dripping down our chins.

Tomatoes rated high with us, as did almost everything that could be eaten raw: carrots wrenched up out of the ground and washed under the pump, so orange and crisp—crunch-crunch-crunch . . . tough, stringy stalks of rhubarb so painfully sour they made the jaws complain even when stabbed into a fistful of salt ("pieplant," it was also called; with lots of sugar it made a tangy sauce and heavenly pies whose juice bubbled sunset-pink.) . . . turnips so white and purple they looked like painted clowns . . . muskmelon (or cantaloupe) split open with a jack-knife, the seeds scooped out, the sweet, pale orange flesh engorged clear down to the lime-green rind.

But nothing could surpass a tomato picked and eaten, still sun-hot, on a drowsy summer's afternoon. And no fragrance is more pungent than that of tomato vines when you brush against them in the dewy dusk playing Hide-and-Go-Seek, or Run, Sheep, Run. The branches were bowed with the scarlet globes; and when they could bear no more you gathered them into bushel baskets and lugged them into the kitchen where other, spicier fragrances were making their contribution to the aroma which claimed the neighborhood: catsup, pickles, chili sauce, relishes. A big cob fire would be roaring, and on the back of the stove Mason jars would be clicking and whispering like people gossiping. Dad would tighten the jars at night when he was home, while Mother took proud inventory: "Fifteen quarts of tomato sauce, nine jars of catsup and five pints of piccalilli!" The rest of us would gloat with her; and as this provender joined the glassy ranks that marched across our dampish, moldy-smelling cellar shelves, a feeling of peace and plenty would overtake us: a snug and squirrel-like sense of conquest and provision against the winter's cold.

Vegetables weren't all that made summer such a halcyon time for a child. There was the fruit as well. Beginning with a fairyland of bloom in the spring (the fat pink apple blossoms, the lacy parasols of cherries and plums), it progressed through tantalizing stages to become luxuriant desserts that clotted the fences, burdened the trees, and rained in wanton plenty upon the ground. And the children were greedily in tune to every stage: "There's cherries big as acorns on the tree!" "The apples are getting ripe!" While parents admonished, "Not yet, it'll be another week at least. Now you kids be careful. Remember how sick you got last year."

It must have begun in Eden, for the lure of a forbidden apple is eternal and intense. I regret that my own children have never known its thrill or suffered its particular bellyache, for about it was an aura of derring-do. Reversing the role of Eve, a boy would scramble up the tree, biting joyously into the prize and describing its delights to more timorous girls below. Then he would toss a few down, or shake the tree, so that you literally had to duck temptation's fusillade. And the tartness when you yielded, the sour juices of your sin, only made it the more sweet. . . .

Tiny crab apples, sometimes worm-riddled. Jonathans, Winesaps, Wealthies, in vivid and varied shades of red. And Grimes Golden and Golden Delicious, hard and yellow as the Apples of Hesperides for which Hercules braved the dragon (much as we braved parents), but ripening to a melting mealiness. . . .

And the plums, great purple ellipses, frosted with a misty coating and gummed with little drops of juice where you rooted them out of the wet, tangled grass. . . . Grapes in drunken clusters on the fence, ready to be transformed by mothers into delicious substances—juice and jams and jellies, but with plenty for a child to eat, sucking the winy juice and eschewing the sour green "eyeballs" in the middle, and spewing out the seeds. . . . And the gaudy rubies of the cherries gemming the trees.

You had to combat the sharp brambly twigs to get at

the cherries, and it was always a race with the birds. Grandpa made marvelous scarecrows; they were almost as gay as his snowmen, with their whimsical touches of glasses, pipe, and cane, but they didn't fool the thieving jays and blackbirds and cedar waxwings. Though birds and children stuffed themselves, there was still plenty for pies and preserves.

There were ground cherries too, half-fruit, half-vegetable, nesting on the ground, to be opened like little tissue paper packages, with one lone yellow pearl inside. And plump rose-red strawberries. And blackberries as fat as your thumb. And seedy but velvety raspberries, soft as a pussy willow in the spring—soft as Daisy's nose—so velvety soft they melted on your tongue.

We ate our way through summer, from the first crisp garden carrots to the peanuts we roasted in the bonfires of fall. No competition from Good Humor men; no adult voices urging, "Now eat your vegetables, take your vitamins." Blissfully unaware, we gobbled and gorged ourselves on nature's raw fresh offerings and were as healthy as colts. When there was a pump handy we washed our plunder. If not, we ate it anyway, cheerfully reasoning, "You've got to eat a peck of dirt before you die." There was little danger, for nobody sprayed against rivals then. Just as we didn't begrudge the bees their honey, we didn't begrudge a few apples to the worms. If we found an intruder, biting down, we simply threw the fruit away, and reached for more. . . .

I dream sometimes of those abundant summers in memory's lost emerald land of Oz. I wish my children could make little boats out of new-picked pods, and eat green apples, and raid a watermelon patch. I wish they

could wake up some morning and find a scarecrow grinning at them from a bird-ringing cherry tree.

Since they can't, I want them to know that fruits and
vegetables don't grow on the shelves of a supermarket,
to be had solely for money and the opening of packages.
That somewhere they are being born and harvested by
human hands out of God's own earth and sky and sun and
rain.

III

Whatever Happened to Run, Sheep, Run?

Whatever happened, I sometimes wonder, to Hide-and-Seek? And Pump, Pump, Pull-Away, as we called it. And Old Gray Wolf? And where, oh, where are the children who used to trample gardens, clamber over fences, and shatter the quiet darkness with their cries of "Run, sheep, run!" They're now suburban housewives like me, I suppose, or busy commuting dads. And their offspring are just as eager as we were to play out-of-doors after supper, and no doubt just as stricken by the stern, inevitable voices of parents calling them in.

You can hear them now at their games of kickball (a marvelous version of baseball) in the street. Or they have bike races. They play war. And they're mad about something called Muck-a-Ny, involving two teams and played with either hands or a ball, a kind of tag. One day they'll probably wax nostalgic about all these for their own bemused, mystified young.

But Hide-and-Seek? To them it's an indoor activity associated with closets and kitchen doors when they were little kids. Old Gray Wolf? Never heard of it. And what was Run, Sheep, Run?

It's just as well not to tell them. For they dare not rove as we did, often for blocks and blocks in the dreamy security of our little town. And where in all suburbia would they find the wonderful places to hide? The woodsheds and gullies, the icehouse, the few remaining haymows, and all the enthralling nooks and crannies of the vast, deserted Chautauqua pavilion in the cool, tree-studded park . . .

The crowds began to gather right after supper, in that lovely twilight hour just before the streetlamps came on. Fathers had just begun to rock on porches over the evening paper, the acrid tang of their pipes and cigars blending with the lingering odor of pot roast and the fragrances of new-cut lawns. Mothers joined them shortly, still drying their hands from the dishes. And little girls, with a final swipe at the sink or the kitchen floor, tore wildly out to join their brothers, already gravitated to the corner streetlight, focal point of almost all our games.

The boys, noisy, belligerent, spitting, would be winding lazily about on their bikes, or standing eyeball-to-eyeball battling it out as to who was to be It. Sometimes they welcomed us roundly, sometimes they scorned us, in which case we flounced off to somebody's yard to play Redlight, Giant Steps, or Statue—a glorious fandango in which a strong-armed kid would grab you and hurl you as far as he could. You then froze into positions of sculptured grace from which he chose the best. It was then your turn.

Occasionally a boy or two would condescend to join us in these milder contests. And their sterner voices commanding, "Redlight!" as you crept forward, step by step—

their stronger arms flinging you in Statue, or yanking you from base in another favorite ("Pump, pump, pull-away, if you don't come I'll pull you away!"), both intensified and vaguely spoiled our fun.

But mostly boys hung around the corner, hitting, wrestling, arguing, pitching pocketknives at the already battle-scarred lamppost—knowing, no doubt, as males usually do, that we'd soon come panting back and beg to play with them on whatever terms they set. Sometimes they even summoned us, for the more kids you had, the better —especially when it came to teams for our wild running and hiding games.

Anyway, once we all got together, the whole business of counting out and choosing sides had to be done. Only the meek and unimaginative fell back on the old familiar "Eenie-Meenie" method of counting out. Older, tougher hands came up with "Monkey, monkey, bottle of beer," or "One potato, two potato, three potato, *four!*"

One that vastly impressed me was "Ocka bocka." Ocka bocka was introduced by a boy named Russell, newly moved to our neighborhood from Fort Dodge. Russell looked just like Rudolph Valentino, and all the girls were madly in love with him. Russell had us stand in a circle and hold out both fists, which he struck with a very dazzling and citified air as he chanted, "Ocka bocka, stona crocka, ocka bocka *boo!* . . . Put that hand behind you!" It took twice as long and seemed very knowing and sophisticated, and I dreamed about him every night.

It having been determined, we'd all taunt, "Yer It, yer It, you've got a fit and don't know how to get out of it!" as he buried his face against the faithful lamppost and began to count. That was signal enough for us to tear off through the gathering dusk to hide.

Actually, to be *It* wasn't so bad. Especially if you were playing Old Gray Wolf. Which, as I recall, was simply a louder, lustier version of Hide-and-Seek. You hid in couples (I was always dying to get Russell) and on rare occasions might get kissed. Also, instead of yelling, "Here I come, ready or not," *It* announced his intentions by imitating a wolf. *It* was free to howl, snarl, bay, whine, or otherwise vent his lupine personality as he prowled for prey. And the rest of us were supposed to mock and echo, albeit faintly, as we maneuvered slyly back toward base.

I marvel that so many parents were able to withstand this eerie rending of their evening's calm; and I really can't blame the Duvals, who considered themselves very superior and refined, for refusing to allow their children to join in our bloody-sounding goings-on.

All our favorite games involved hiding and mystery and pursuit, culminating in a violent chase. But the one that really sent us was Run, Sheep, Run. For this you chose up two sides, with a captain for each. One band would remain at the lamppost, while the other slipped away in search of some new, impregnable, totally unsuspected hiding place. Up alleys, across back fences, through vacant lots, backtracking so as to leave no clues.

We skirted the prim, well-tended premises of the Duvals, where Judith and LeRoy, poor things, would be safely reading *National Geographic,* or playing Flinch, or getting ready for bed. Sometimes they would watch wistfully from windows or dare to call down to us. And awareness of their imprisonment added to our sense of abandon in our dark, devilish adventure and intrigue.

Everybody wanted to be captain. The captain got to make up the signals and call them out importantly. If he were the phlegmatic sort he settled for dull, ordinary code

words—like "catsup," or "onion stew." Others were wildly inventive, rhythmic, and often funny: "Now if I holler 'Baby ate the preacher' that'll mean don't worry, we're going the other direction. But if I yell, 'Dynamite the schoolhouse,' that'll mean lay low, get down. 'Join the circus!' will mean here we come, get ready to run . . ."

Plotting and conspiring, we huddled together in the finally chosen den—a culvert, Redenbaughs' woodpile, a cellar with slanting doors through which you could peek, a barn, a garage, behind the pillars of the yawning park pavilion. Then the captain would circle back to confront the enemy, crossing his index fingers to indicate the directions in which we might be. Taut, we listened for his first vital signal informing us of their choice. But we were not free to move until we heard his further alarms, warnings, and messages, no matter how far the foe might be led astray.

In a bliss of fear, suspense, anticipation, we waited, listening—listening. . . . Stars glittered overhead. Frogs thumped their deep bass fiddles in the rushes along the lake. Crickets and locusts chirred and racketed in the trees. Bats swooped low. A player piano poured its liquid music into the street. A slow freight rumbled through town—you could sometimes hear the doomed livestock bawling in their slatted cars, and catch a sour-sweet whiff. There was the lonely barking of dogs. The whole night was strange, delicious with danger.

Signals dimmed in the distance, or drew nearer. Shuddering, we clutched each other at the approaching footsteps, the voices speculating. Then at last the final signal, the glorious release. They had tracked us down or were hot on the trail: "Run, sheep, run!" Screaming like wild horses, we came tearing out of our hiding place, not sheep at all, but frantic creatures pounding madly home. For your goal, the sole center of your existence, was that serenely shining beacon on the distant corner, the pale and patient streetlamp.

By now the gnats and mosquitoes would be swarming there in circles, as numerous as the children. Moths hurled themselves blindly to destruction in that sturdy lady's burning eye beneath her scalloped hat. And there were great night beetles—June bugs we called them—fat and shiny, that fell with horrible plopping clicks. If the boys suspected your revulsion, they would drop them, scratching and kicking, down your back.

Now it was the other side's turn to hide. And it was almost as exciting to try to figure out their signals and trail them to their lair. Hot and sweaty from our run, we trudged the town, often in vehement argument with their leader, always alert to his tricks. Drinking great draughts of the night air, rich with its smell of clover and trampled grass and dirty kids. Wishing on falling stars—or scaring ourselves with tales of death and dark portents.

And always, long before you had had enough, parental voices began calling you in. You heard them no matter how far you had ranged, or scouts announced your doom. "Hey, your mother's calling—"

In a frenzy of frustration, you pleaded, implored—in vain. "You heard me. Go get the others, tell them I mean it now!" Rounding up brothers and sisters postponed the sentence a few minutes longer. But soon we were all straggling across the grass, toward the coal of Dad's cigar, where he sat on the creaking, chain-hung porch swing behind the vines. Like the light on the corner, it made a cheerful glow.

Mother would often have a big cut-glass pitcher of lemonade, tartly sweet, and cool to our burning throats. Its ice had been chopped from the big square chunk in the wooden box, and we sat sucking it to slivers when the lemonade was gone.

Or we would crouch on the porch steps a little longer, hoping desperately that we hadn't missed Mr. Wilson's candy wagon, making its final tour along the leafy streets. It was one of the few horse-drawn conveyances I recall from those lost days—almost everything else was trucks and cars; but the candy wagon lent a kind of old-world dignity and magic as it plodded and creaked along.

And listening for those plocking hooves, the grating of its wheels, enduring the awful suspense of wondering whether you'd be given the necessary nickel to stop it, equaled and possibly surpassed that of huddling in the darkness listening for the signals of your Leader. If Dad reached in his pocket, out we'd all rush, waving our arms, and Mr. Wilson would stop, and from the shadowy recesses of his canvas curtains, produce those treats that never seem to change—ice-cream cones or candy bars. . . .

Thank goodness! It's nice to know there are a few pleasures that bridge the generations, that don't mystify and amuse my progeny when I speak of "bygone days." They think it sad and rather funny that we didn't have air conditioning and freezers and TV and space flights. They'll never understand the thrill of the space flights we took almost every night on long summer evenings: up alleys, over fences, through gardens and yards and the starry park, playing Run, Sheep, Run!

IV

All Doors Led to the Kitchen

I am a modern woman and my kitchen is my pride. I'm glad I don't have to build a fire in the cookstove or nag a son to carry out the ashes. I enjoy my Formica and chrome, my efficient planning unit, my shining salad center and dessert bar. It's great to be mistress of a panel that would do credit to a cockpit and have all these gadgets that start cooking and cleaning and freezing and grinding at a touch. I *guess* I appreciate the fan that whisks away the aroma of my Chicken Cacciatore or Swordfish Foo Yung. And if I pine for the company of my offspring, I can contact them on their intercom, or set the timer on my oven and join them in the family room.

But I warmly recall the days of the big, smelly, noisy, inconvenient kitchen, short on cupboard space but long on living. Days when the kitchen *was* the family room, hub and heart of the house.

Most families were bigger then (if you had only one or two children you were considered snobs), and when a man built his house he made sure it had plenty of kitchen. There was also a "front room" and, if he wanted to put on

the dog, a double-doored parlor where company was entertained. But all doors led inevitably back to the enormous
teeming kitchen. For here practically every activity occurred—cooking, eating, reading, washing, ironing, playing games, and sometimes sleeping, for it wasn't uncom-
mon for the kitchen to include a couch.

Undisputed queen of this kitchen was the big black
range. It warmed you, cooked your meals, heated your
bath water and the flatirons with which your mother
ironed your clothes. It also had a lot to do with her dis-
position. For in those days a woman's relationship to her
stove had an intimacy, a quality of involvement that can
never be duplicated by simply turning a switch for elec-
tricity or gas. The cookstove was almost human. When its
belly was full and it was roaring away in a cheery mood,
so was your mother, most likely. She sang as she worked.
But when the stove sulked or smoked, refused to heat the
oven, or went out, it was like some awful personal feud.

Stoves sometimes lasted for generations. Because
Mother inherited hers from her mother-in-law, they were
rivals from the start. She blamed it for every cooking fail-
ure. Finally, when it was a draw as to who was more
temperamental, Mother or the range, Dad began to save
and plan and together they explored the stores and studied
the catalogs. The whole family was in a state of excited
anticipation.

How regal the new stove looked when it was finally
lifted off the dray. Its plump arched feet seemed almost
too refined for the worn linoleum, its nickel-plated scrolls
and curlicues too elegant. It had a big oven, two handsome warming closets, and two fancy little shelves to set
pans on. Joy of Mother's life, it had a reservoir bulging
like a growth on its side. When this was filled with water

from the scrawking cistern at the sink you could dip soft warm water for baths any time the stove was hot.

Dad carefully fitted the tin chimney pipe together, and it went curving into the wall graceful as a dancer stretching. The boys, who usually had to be nagged, vied to help build the fire using the new tools—poker, lid lifter, and a little curved gadget to shake down the ashes. Soon the flames of life were licking cheerily through the new-comer, and Mother was frying chicken to celebrate.

"Oh, I'm going to keep it so nice," she cried. "I just love my new stove."

It settled down in time to being one of us. Despite Mother's ardent forays with stove blacking, its impressive countenance faded, from much spilling and scrubbing, to a comfortable pink. When you treated it right it would sing and cluck to you and rattle its clinkers, and its cheeks would glow rosy as a girl's. You could see its red heart shining through its grate. But it would always remain the autocrat of the kitchen, a kind of royal adjunct of your mother, on whom the comforts of life depended.

The day always started with the stove. There was the pound of feet on the back stairs as Dad or a brother went down to cope with it. The rattle of shaken ashes, the crack of kindling, the click of lids, the clatter of coal—such was the first music of morning. Though sometimes Dad laid the fire the night before. Then all he had to do was give it a dollop of kerosene, toss a match, and boom! Flames would go tearing up the chimney, yelling like the merry fiends of hell.

Mother frowned on this procedure, but it was fast. By the time the kids had been hounded out of bed, grabbed their clothes and dashed downstairs to dress, the tea-kettle would be rocking and spitting, the coffee boiling

richly in its chipped granite pot, and the fragrance of thick bacon or side meat filling the house.

The kitchen range engorged a vast amount of fuel. Beside it sat the snout-mouthed coal pail filled with glittering nuggets from which the poker jutted gaily, like a spear. Behind that was a round peach basket heaped with dry mealy cobs; behind that the woodbox. Dad was forever ordering more cobs, which a farmer would dump into a lovely red or white mountain out by the woodshed. "There's nothing like a cob fire," Mother always said. "It's quick and clean and hot." Brothers were forever being driven forth to haul in more. Or to chop more kindling, lug in more coal. They were always carrying something—fuel, water, ashes.

I never envied those reluctant young beasts of burden, boys. Though there was something appealing about the ashes, drawn in their oblong pan from the deep recesses of the stove. Ashes were velvety soft and gray as pussy willows; they gave off a wispy dust and, when hot, an acrid smell. They often held "clinkers," cinders that refused to melt into silvery nothingness but remained like stubbornly contorted bodies, tough and gleaming. There was something clean, spare, and triumphant about the pan when it had been emptied out by the alley; even the boy's step was jauntier, returning. And when the pan was slid, with a gritting sound, back into the yawning vacancy, there was a brief sense of newness and beginning. A joyous readiness to receive.

For times when you didn't want to build a fire there was the oil stove. It took dainty, vaguely distasteful sips of kerosene and gave off a tart smell, unlike the big aromatic range. It was tall-chimneyed and aloof and somehow annoyed with the lot of us, as if it knew it played second fiddle. Through its isinglass doors flickered pointy blue tongues of flame. When you forgot to trim the wicks it sputtered and smoked. It was efficient and quick, but it lacked the expansiveness, the embracing grandeur and vitality of the big cookstove.

Second only in importance to the kitchen stove was the kitchen table. No breakfast nooks for us, no perching on stools at a snack bar. Instead, just as the stove drew you with its warmth, the table drew you to its broad, hospitable bosom. A huge walnut table, usually, sometimes round, sometimes square, and covered by oilcloth.

Here, rushing in after school, you found your mother kneading the slippery, squeaky white bread dough, or setting out the tall brown, heavenly smelling loaves to cool. Or she would be rolling out piecrust or pitting cherries for canning. Whatever her labors, there was always room to spread out your books, your kites, your paper dolls, or your treasures of rocks and leaves and wild flowers. Here, munching whatever it was she was cooking, the two of you visited.

By some legerdemain our mother managed to remove all this and set that same table for supper if Dad wasn't home. (When he was, or if we had company, she used the dishes from the glass china closet instead of the pantry, and we ate in the dining room.) And afterward, she got the dishpans from their nails on the back porch, and there too the dishes were washed. Then when all this was cleared away, the real activities of the evening began:

The homework—the singsong of multiplication tables, the drill on spelling words accompanied by a little chorus of outdoor sounds. Crickets and katydids beyond the screen, a barking dog. Rain at the windows, or the soft, almost audible silence of snow. Or wind that rattled shutters, made the panes squeal with dancing branches, and puffed the rag rugs Mother had put against the doorsills to keep it out. All of this sheltered and cupped in the kitchen, still steamy and redolent of supper, with the range clucking and whispering away like a companionable old nanny.

And after the lessons, the games. Pit or Old Maid or the agonizingly exciting Flinch. Dad taught us rummy, which Mother enjoyed but worried about because we used real playing cards. ("Instruments of the devil," ministers called them, pounding the pulpit—and here they were, wickedly black and red and gay against our shiny oilcloth.)

"Now, Mama, forget it," Dad chuckled. "So long as we don't gamble—"

"Well—" in shy but reckless triumph—"I've got a book, I've got three queens!"

Somebody always got hungry, and there was always a discussion whether to stir up the fire and add more fuel, or let it die down and use the coals. We made a batch of fudge, which bubbled richly until the precise moment when it "spun a thread," then was beaten lengthily on the cold, enclosed back porch, and cut in mealy squares and served still in the buttery pie tin. Or cups of scalding black cocoa, with marshmallows melting in a foamy gum on top. Or we toasted the marshmallows that Dad brought home in a striped candy sack over the rosy intensity of the coals.

Sometimes we roasted apples in these fiercely glowing pink coals. Despite the time they took, they never got done in the middle and no amount of sugar, cream, or spices could ever make them taste like anything to me but dumb old baked apples. The coals were marvelous, though, for toasting bread. You pinioned it on a long-handled fork, held it, standing back, until the sudden instant of its golding. A second longer might burn it into a cinder—but to snatch it back and butter it now meant perfection. The outside crisp, the inside tender, and the whole of it subtly flavored with the breath of fire.

The most frequent treat was popcorn. The black-screen corn popper hung on a handy hook. The sound and the smell of the white imps dancing as if eager to join us added to our pleasure. You could see them jumping to get out. Then when the popper could hold no more they were released into a dishpan, slathered with salt and butter, and eaten by the handful.

Mother had an anecdote about popcorn—half joke, half foolish confession: "I ate an entire dishpan full of popcorn *all by myself* the night before each of you were born."

The fun was enlivened if one or two grade school friends were with us. Perhaps because this was rare. The place for younger children then was home. No running over to Sally's to do your homework together—there also to listen to records and talk on the phone. When we were small, our Victrola remained in the parlor which was rather chilly and not friendly like the kitchen. And the big wooden wall phone, though it hung in the kitchen, rang so infrequently by night that when it did everybody was startled, thinking something was wrong. Nor were people always racing around by car. If a girl was so lucky as to spend an evening in your family circle, she came with her brother (it was often why you asked her). Or your own brother put on his cap and walked her home.

Certainly at night parents were not always off at parties or meetings. Nobody had ever heard of a babysitter. If "the folks" simply had to go somewhere, they packed up the kids and took them along. But mostly they too were home—and not off in a basement workshop, or immersed in papers at a desk, or absorbed in their hobbies, but in the big sprawling kitchen where everybody gravitated. And to exclude them from your activities would be unthinkable. In fact, if they did actually prefer to read or sew or attend to other pursuits we were shocked and grieved. Didn't they appreciate our fascinating company? We knew that without theirs we felt deprived.

For when night fell and the supper dishes were cleared away, it was as if a kind of happy magic invaded the house, and its focus was the kitchen table. There Mother seemed to shed her cares along with her apron. She became lively, pretty—even witty. While that worried and often grim authority, Dad, turned into an outright clown.

The kitchen table was also sometimes utilized for more serious purposes. A man down the street had an attack of appendicitis, and the doctor whacked his appendix out right there—on the kitchen table.

The kitchens of my childhood usually had a sink stuck off in a corner used mainly for peeling potatoes, or a quick washing up. If you had city water, its pipe arched rather contemptuously over the old granite basin Dad kept there along with his strong hand soap. It was like a skinny-necked aristocrat with a spigot-bow on her brow. If you were rich there were two of these spare maidens, one for hot. The real boss of the sink was the cistern pump. When you grabbed its squatty handle and jerked up and down it made tortured sounds, often so dry and gasping you had to prime it with sips from a pitcher. As if to soothe and encourage, "Now you try." Finally it would begin to gurgitate—spurts of soft water, wonderful for

washing dishes and clothes and especially hair. The hard
city water curdled the soap and could chap your hands.
Lots of people refused even to drink the city water; it
tasted funny after the cold purity of the well outdoors.
Pumps might be old-fashioned, and the cistern humble and
homely, but you sensed, as it grumbled and gushed, that
by golly it knew its worth.

Another major character in the cast of the kitchen
was the brown varnished icebox. It squatted, thickly im-
passive, near the door to be handy to the iceman. Hearing
the jingle of harness or plock of hooves up the shady street,
Mother would open the top lid, make a quick inspection,
and send one of us out to tell Johnny Peterson how many
pounds today. The Petersons were a big German family
who drove teams onto the frozen lake and hewed the ice
with giant saws. Their castle-high icehouses were land-
marks along the windy shore.

Other kids would already be swarming the hooded
wagon, begging or snatching bright slivers and chunks to
suck. You weren't supposed to eat the raw ice or even put
it in lemonade, considering its source, but everybody did.
Grabbing a block with the jaws of his mighty tongs,
Johnny would haul it toward him and split it cleanly with
a pick, or cut it neat as a great glassy cake with his saw.
Then slosh! went his bucket of water to rinse the sawdust
off, and he'd heave it to his shoulder and stagger, a kind
of Atlas, toward the house.

The icebox was strong, cold, impersonal despite its
contents. Its only sound was the soft drip of water into the
pan lodged beneath its feet discreetly behind a wooden
flap. The icebox understood that you loved the stove better,
or the table, but who did you come to when the stove
was out and nobody else was around? It! It never told

when you ate the last piece of pie or chicken; it just sat there and dripped.

Just off the kitchen a little pantry was tacked on. Here your mother kept not only her everyday dishes and most of her supplies but the entire accouterment of her cooking. And her dearest dream was to own a kitchen cabinet. How prosaic a name for so impressive a furnishing. For it was to any kitchen what a piano was to a parlor—it lent class. Tall and lovely it stood, two frosted glass doors concealing an enticing array of shelves and little compartments. Below this was a small work surface, and below that drawers and bins. Its *pièce de résistance* was the flour dispenser. By turning a little crank out came a cone of already sifted flour!

What wizardry! What a time-saver! Then, as now, women suddenly realized how desperately they needed something they had not known existed before. Mother was miserable with longing from the moment she saw one, and Dad miserable on her behalf. Taking us slyly into the secret, he began to save for one. All winter he saved, hoping to have enough for the new one in the furniture store window in time for her birthday in May. Then in March, ironically, working on the ice for Johnny Peterson to add a little extra to the fund, he broke his leg. No health insurance in those days. Every cent had to go for grocery bills and doctor bills. It was the first time I had ever seen my father cry.

He was still on crutches in April when the family down the street decided to sell out and move to Omaha. Hearing the news, Dad hobbled off hopefully: Mrs. Marshall had a kitchen cabinet! Presently the telephone rang. "Now don't say anything to Mama, but get your brothers down here right away with a couple of coaster wagons."

Fortunately, Mother was off at Ladies Aid. I ran all over the neighborhood trying to round up my brothers, and finally wound up borrowing a wagon and hauling one of them myself. The men had taken the cabinet apart. They reassembled it in our kitchen, working fast so as to have it done by the time Mother got home.

She came up the sidewalk, all dressed up and looking radiant, the way she always did after an afternoon out. I'll never forget our prancing excitement, hiding behind the door to watch. Or the look of mystification on her face. Followed by such amazement she had to sit down. "I don't believe it. A kitchen—*cabinet!*"

It far surpassed the night she finally got her stove.

This cabinet proved to have less convenience than class, alas. But she doted on it, arranging and rearranging it for hours. The stove would always be the old dowager queen, but the cabinet graced the kitchen like a glamorous princess. . . .

Children will always be excited by anything new in the house. But today's affluence and installment buying have robbed us of the drama, the longing hope, the sacrifice —the suspense. If you want something today you just go out and buy it. How can objects so acquired have personality? And how can food seem vital when it is no longer related to the elements once so real to us—fire and ice and water physically produced? How can a kitchen be emotionally significant when it is only an efficient, if attractive, laboratory? A place where Mother punches buttons, opens package mixes, or defrosts different dinners for people to eat in different places if they want to watch different programs.

I sometimes wish that we could all be whisked back

together in time. That my children would have to chop wood, haul water, build a fire before they could eat or bathe or even have clean clothes. Above all, I wish they could draw their chairs into the snug circle around the kitchen table after supper, when the day's chores were done and everybody was ready for Flinch and fudge and popcorn. Ready for the comfort and pleasure of each other's company, while the wind snooped round the door and the rosy coals of the old cookstove clucked like a benediction on the grate.

V

The Days of Movie Magic

"What's on TV?" one teen-ager asks. And the other reads the program, a varied menu of comedy, drama, concerts, movies, and documentaries. Both keep offering objections —one's not in color, that one's a rerun, or "Yuck! Who can stand that dame? What's playing at the movies?"

Mother's already checked. "Nothing fit for you to see." They don't fight it. Besides, sex poured on in buckets can eventually lose its allure. Mother picks up the paper and contributes to the evening's possibilities: There's the Ice Capades. The symphony. The ballet. Danny Kaye in person. Shakespeare. A Broadway musical. The box office generally has a few spares; the money can be managed. But the very plethora of potentials defeats their interest. They decide to go bowling.

We had no such problems when I was growing up. You simply went to the show. Mike Tracy's Empire Theatre with its stale yet thrilling air, smelling of popcorn, gum wrappers, and delight. If you got there early you could grab one of the prized front seats. Here those gods of the silver screen loomed so close they could almost literally dissolve you into their dream world. Also, you could watch the piano player gazing intently at the screen, interpreting. Miss Woodruff was best, a magnificent woman who gave voice and elocution lessons. She was a born entertainer, our local Cornelia Otis Skinner. And when she took over a piano her whole body engaged itself in joyful combat, while the very ribbon on her pince-nez flew like a pennant. In exciting parts she practically mounted that piano and whipped it right up onto the screen to join the chase.

Or just before the lights went out one of the high school girls would saunter down the aisle, smooth her skirts, and arrange her music. Joyce Kaufman or maybe Julia Zwickey. We were awed and envious. Imagine getting to see a show free every night, and even being paid!

Then Mr. Hazuke's projector would start to hum, and a shining sword cut through the velvety darkness, severing you from the dull world of everyday. First a newsreel. Then the main picture. Then a comedy. The Pathé newsreel started with a rooster crowing, and wound up with a cameraman, cap on backwards, still cranking. In the newsreel you saw interesting things from all over the world: the Prince of Wales, Chinese rickshaws, a Boy Scout meeting President Coolidge. The comedy was always slapstick, with custard pies in faces and much racing down railroad tracks in carts frantically propelled by the Keystone Cops, Our Gang, or Harold Lloyd.

During all this Mike Tracy, a kindly, bemused little Irishman, would prowl the aisles keeping order and throwing out any kids who tried to sneak in via the alley Exit. Though most of us were too enthralled to misbehave.

Sometimes, astoundingly, instead of the comedy the lights came on and the curtain rolled down, with its ads for the bank, the feedstore, the lumberyard, the funeral parlor. Vaudeville! We were mad with surprise and joy. Tumblers. A juggler. A comedian. A team of soft-shoe dancers. One couple had a daughter who sang "Yes, Sir, That's My Baby" in a harsh-sweet stagy voice. My friend Aleda's mother sold tickets at the show, and Aleda not only got to go free every night, she met these dazzling people. The highlight of one summer was getting to play paper dolls all one afternoon with Aleda and this awesome child of the stage.

The show was on every night except Sunday, and the theater, so bleakly locked, added to the melancholy of the day. The week's program was printed on handbills that we snatched from the porch eagerly. Our whole family always went Wednesday nights because Mother was already dressed up for Ladies Aid. That it was a school night never bothered anybody; we had blessedly little homework, and anyway we went to the first show. Afterward the suspense was agonizing—would Dad lead us all into The Greek's? The Greek's confectionery was also known as The Candy Kitchen. Here the divine fragrance of the chocolates they made in back mingled with the chill enticements of sundaes. Sometimes we sat down richly at the little round marble tables to make painful choices from the menu's heady poesy: Hawaiian Sunset. Pike's Peak Surprise. Sometimes the limit was fifty cents worth of the candy tantalizing in its glass case. Sometimes, despite pleas and exhortations, we must only march stoically past. Dad suffered most; his nature was loving and lavish. He never failed to dig down at least for candy bars, which we munched blissfully, still in the thrall of the show, walking home under the stars.

We went by ourselves to the Saturday matinee. The

serials held us captive. (Pearl White was always left dangling from a cliff or tied to railroad tracks.) And when you got older a boy might walk you home from the show, or even self-consciously pay your way. A date really *meant* going to the show.

We learned about life from the show. Sweet romance from the Gish sisters or Mary Pickford. Adventure from Douglas Fairbanks (that flashing smile, those daring leaps!). Steely-eyed courage from William S. Hart. Passion from Theda Bara, John Gilbert, Rudolph Valentino, Greta Garbo. Silent Stars of the Silver Screen—a multitude of the heavenly hosts that began to shine through our lives from infancy.

We worshiped them as gods, cut out their pictures to pin on bedroom walls, pored over movie magazines, reading how Pola Negri took milk baths and kept a pet tiger, but Marguerite Clarke was as simple as the girl next door. No sex revelations, ever. When Fatty Arbuckle made questionable headlines he was barred from the movies. Those high priests of Hollywood, D. W. Griffith and Cecil B. DeMille, set the tone for the sociological phenomenon that "picture shows" were. Beyond a few harmless "vamps" on leopard-skin couches, a few Roman orgies in their epics, their movies were pure and the people who played in them were expected to be likewise, at least for public consumption. They had the quaint but wonderful notion that movies bore a moral responsibility.

Certainly we identified with those fabulous beings who created such magic for us, and our behavior was profoundly influenced by what we saw at the show. When Wallace Reed died we were not only grief-stricken but stunned. Dope? Our gay, clean-cut Wally? Impossible! The film his wife made later showing the evils of drugs engraved its awful message on our souls. And when America's sweetheart, Mary Pickford, sued Doug Fairbanks for divorce, we couldn't have been much more shocked if Mother had left Dad.

These people were not only intensely real to us in those small-town, pre-TV days, they were our most vivid models. We tried to copy the worldliness of Gloria Swanson, the wit of Constance Talmadge, the madcap collegiate antics of Clara Bow. The suave male stars were paragons of gallantry and glamour. They even affected our manners. I remember dating a boy whose family generally ate comfortably on oilcloth in the kitchen with Pop sometimes in an undershirt. But the boy's own manners were, by contrast, so impressive I finally summoned the nerve to ask how-come?

Well, he acknowledged sheepishly, he'd made up his mind to be somebody some day. "And I've been watching Ronald Colman. How he always offers his arm to a lady when they go in to dinner, and even stands up when she enters the room—"

By then it was Ronald Colman. Movies had begun to talk! It was the seductive accents of Charles Boyer. The clipped tough-guy tones of Jimmy Cagney. You could even hear him smack a dame. We had a whole new constellation of stars to imitate—in a new way. A curious new code of behavior. For with sound came sin. Situations that would only be suggested before in subtitles and fade-outs became suddenly exciting, immediate, viable. And oh, boy, that Norma Shearer! In films like *Riptide*, or *A Free Soul*. A phrase from the latter still rings in my ears: "From now on my bedroom door will be closed to nobody but my husband!" Wow. But though we sat titillated, and frankly scared, the bedroom doors were always closed before things got too lively.

By comparison with what goes today, those "daring" scenes seem about as spotless as Shirley Temple in *Heidi*. And the Golden Age which followed (when people got mad enough to protest—including Eleanor Roosevelt—and Hollywood was shamed into forming its own Motion Picture Production Code) as remote as the Crusades. For the teeth of the Code were its taboos. They wouldn't let any unmarried couple even set foot inside a bedroom. They even timed the kisses. Which may have been going to extremes, but kept things under control. And still produced stars like March and Cooper and Gable. Like Jeanette MacDonald and Mary Martin and Claudette Colbert . . .

My first crop of children could movie-date as casually as we did. Hold hands, have a hamburger, and come home entertained, often enlightened, at least unharmed. Our final teen-agers seldom go. It's simply too much trouble to check out all the playhouses trying to find something that won't embarrass them with a boy or girl friend. They have no recollection of a time when movies were clean, when you could simply call up a girl and take her to the nearest show.

They think I'm ancient, as is. I don't tell them I remember even before that. When pianos plinked accompaniment. When big kids read the titles aloud to younger ones. When whole families sat transported by a firmament of silent stars.

VI

Give Me
an Old-Fashioned Peddler

Sign of age though it may be, it seems to me that solicitors
and salesmen somehow lack the appeal and flavor they
had when I was a small-town child. Today when my door
chimes echo their insistent summons above the drumming
of the shower, what do I find when I grab a robe and dash
dripping to the door? A lace lady? A scissors grinder?
A chimney sweep? Maybe a gypsy, even?

No, indeed.

I'm rewarded by a neighbor collecting for another
fund. Or a feverish if beaming phony, claiming he must
have my magazine subscriptions within the hour or he'll
lose a scholarship to college. A nicely scrubbed little boy
clutching tickets to the Cub Scout circus. The Fuller Brush
man maybe. The Avon lady or a soulful pitchman for
cemetery lots.

The fact that I don't relish these interruptions puzzles
my children. With the eternal kindness and curiosity of
the young, they'd have me invite the stranger in and send
no one away without having first lightened my purse.

They don't realize that, despite all our "time-saving"

gadgets and contrivances, today's mothers are actually busier in many ways than were their grandmothers. Also, though most communities have laws that attempt to license and thus eliminate many canvassers, we are still besieged by more people in a week's span than our mothers might have seen in a summer.

In my little hometown each day stretched out before the housewife pretty much like the day before. She was glad to pause in her often horrendous labors (scrubbing on a washboard, say, or whaling the daylights out of a rug) and pass the time of day with a peddler while examining his wares. Those who came calling door-to-door —whether regulars like the Jewel Tea man and old blind Mr. Clarke, who sold soap, or the occasional stranger with brooms over his shoulder—were treated like welcome guests.

"Oh, my goodness, here comes the Jewel Tea wagon," my mother would exclaim. "Pick up those papers quick, and just look at this floor!"

Mr. Hix, the Jewel Tea man, didn't seem to notice, sitting at the oilcloth-covered kitchen table, drinking coffee, and passing along gossipy items picked up on his peregrinations, while mother scribbled additional items on her list. We usually trailed him out to his "wagon," which was actually a skinny-wheeled, top-heavy truck. But, to our dazzled eyes and nostrils, its dusky interior, fragrant with spices, cocoa, tea, its air of plenitude and mobility, made it as enchanting as a desert caravan.

Mother, like many women, always had to rationalize what she bought. "Well, now yes, they are a little higher than the stores downtown, but it's so convenient. And they give such nice premiums."

The premiums were the payoff—the real forerunner

of today's trading stamps. She was saving her coupons for a fringed floor lamp.

Another regular was Mrs. Cannon, a large, bosomy, rich-smelling woman who took orders for yard goods, ribbons, and lace. We called her the Lace Lady; she always wore fountains of it at her wrists and throat, or a lacy shirtwaist tucked into a crackling taffeta skirt. The bolts of lace she brought forth from her big black leather satchel and unwound before your eyes—thick creamy ecru stuff for the yokes of nightgowns or the bordering of curtains and tablecloths; exquisite hand embroidery from the Philippines, or a delicate white froth, like snowflakes or spiderwebs.

Mrs. Cannon had jet-black hair—she went to Omaha to have it dyed, people said—a little moustache, furry eyebrows, and bright black friendly eyes. She was a little bit like a plump jolly spider herself, sitting there in her lovely webbed entanglements of lace. From her, Mother bought most of our broad, watered silk hair ribbons. Mrs. Cannon measured them thumb to nose, and slashed them off smartly with a pair of bright blunt scissors that danced at her waist. She then wound them about the sparkling spindles of her jeweled fingers.

The "goods" had to be ordered from her fabulous sample books. Children lived for the day when she would abandon one of these treasuries and pass it on. Their rectangles of precious satin, velvet, woolens, and gingham prints made marvelous dresses for the tiny penny dolls we bedded down in match boxes; and they couldn't be surpassed for curtaining and carpeting a shoebox dollhouse.

Every Saturday, regular as the clock on the Presbyterian church tower, a small boy would come leading Mr. Clarke and his tapping cane to the steps. One week to take your order, the next to deliver it. Nobody really cared

much for his tarry-smelling brown shampoo or his white, faintly stinging hand soap. But "you just can't turn him away."

He was so sweet and kind and feeble and vaguely Biblical, a little child leading him like that. "Imagine going through life in the dark." We couldn't, even when we shut our eyes and groped about.

No, our support of the blind was intimate and personal, and—as we scrubbed virtuously with the unpleasant products—it had the tart-sweet flavor both of penance for our good fortune and of sacrifice.

It was the advent of a stranger, however, that really perked things up. A tramp at the back door was a matter of tender excitement and subtly delicious alarm. Little bells of adventure rang in our blood as Mother bade him join the family for a square meal, or if he were unduly dirty and suspicious, fed him, feeling guilty and unchristian, on the back steps.

We could feel (often smell!) the open roads, the

campfires, the boxcars rumbling through the night while
a train whistle hooted its wild mysterious call. Moved, we
would watch him trudge humbly off, sometimes in an old
coat Mother had dug from the closet, clutching a dollar
bill Dad had forked over.

"We can't spare it, but doggone it, I just couldn't
bear not to," Dad would say, looking sheepish but glowing.
And we'd glow too, sharing the exaltation.

On a rare and memorable occasion we'd have a chimney sweep. Where they came from it's hard to imagine—
Dickens? A fairy tale?

Anyhow, one day a pair of them would appear, as
if by magic, one on each side of the street. Elfish-looking
little men in tall, pointed hats, their white smiles slashing
their sooty faces, gay and a bit terrifying.

They would go squirreling onto a roof and disappear
into the chimney, probing and prodding with their devil-
ish-looking instruments. The chimneys, clotted from years
of wood and coal smoke, would rain down their velvety
black accumulation.

You couldn't invite them in, they were too grimy. But
you carried a pitcher of ice water or lemonade to cool
them after their labors, and they quaffed it with mighty
workings of their Adam's apples. Then off they'd go, dark
imps that had added a dash to the day.

Another event that always shattered the lassitude of
a summer's afternoon would be the arrival of gypsies. Like
a sudden invasion of locusts they would appear in their
huge old touring cars, parking on Main Street, and spilling
in all directions.

"Gypsies!" the news would start rolling from block
to block. "Here come the gypsies."

Some of the more cautious mothers would scoop up

their children, rush inside, and lock the doors. Others more venturesome held their ground as they hosed the porch or weeded the garden.

Down the street the gypsies would come on foot, the women's bright skirts swishing around their dirty ankles, beads and bracelets jingling. Dark eyes glowed with a sullen mocking fire as they begged, "Silver. Cross my palm with silver, I tell your fortune lady—you going to take a trip, make big fortune."

The voice was dusky like the face, threatening but alluring. We were nearly ill with longing to know its secrets. For these wild people out of nowhere, did they not possess some magic key?

One of them squatted once and took my hand in her hot, dry, wrinkled one and began tracing the lifeline thrillingly. But learning there was no money with which to pay her, rose and spat, and turned away.

Mother said you mustn't encourage them, and *never* let them in the house. People vied later in matching tales of gypsies, their horse thieving and child snatching. But the appearance of these errant invaders heightened the rest of the day.

Less spectacular but always diverting were the men who sharpened knives and scissors on their portable grinding wheels. And the genteel young ladies who took orders for the *Book of Knowledge.* Commonplace but perhaps jolliest of all were the broom peddlers.

"Brooms for sale . . . nice, new brooms!" the broom peddler would call, humping along under the burden of his heavy, bright bouquet. He carried them over his shoulder, those homely wheat-colored whiskery flowers. And what a fine business he did.

The money was counted out and the man trudged

on. There you were with the new broom smelling dry and oaty, to be straddled and ridden, making a fine swish, and leaking a few loose golden strands across the floor.

Your mother would dubiously try it out, struggling with its frisky newness like a horse to be trained. Her eyes would have a kind of wistful twinkling as she said, "It's funny, but I sort of hate to break in a new broom—you get so used to the old one."

You knew what she meant. There was something almost human about a broom. The new one occupied the position of prestige on the hook behind the kitchen door; the old one—lopsided, worn down but dependable—was demoted now to porch or sidewalk sweeping, or the brushing off of snowy boots come wintertime. You hoped the old one didn't mind . . .

Some things never change. We had then, as now, the perennial parade of small boys and girls selling seeds and postcards and subscriptions (and took our own exciting

turns at the ringing of doorbells). Before long we began to have our Fuller Brush men, our Avon ladies, our assaults of young people "working their way" through colleges that have never heard of them. Gradually, something began to be missing, there I'm sure as well as here in suburbia today; the flavor and juice of the old-time interruptions. The sense of expectation, welcome, and surprise. But most of all, a sense of personal involvement with these briefly passing lives.

My children, however eager, can't really enjoy seeing me cope with all these people, as I proclaim in some desperation: "No, no, I cannot use any more brushes, beauty products, magazines, or cemetery lots."

I'd like to fling open the door some day and find a genuine blind man tapping up the steps. Or an old-fashioned smelly hobo to be fed and warmed and sent on his way . . . Or a lady with ribbons and laces . . . A peddler of brooms . . . A gypsy—a chimney sweep!

VII

Every Child Was King
...in a Swing

Today, many a child who has a yard to play in also is the casual possessor of his own "playground set." This is a very efficient and ingenious combination of poles and chains upon which are arranged excellent if somewhat smaller editions of much of the equipment to be found on regulation playgrounds—swings, seesaws, rings, trapezes, and often a slide.

When I was a child in Storm Lake, to have such marvels on your own doorstep would be like having rubbed Aladdin's lamp. Such equipment as we had with which to vent our boundless energies we mostly contrived out of rope, old boards, and imagination. Or for the really polished pleasure we took a leisurely jaunt to the park.

There was an old wooden bandstand in the park, later replaced by a stone bandshell. There was an iron pump that gushed icy water which you drank from Cracker Jack boxes. It also had a hole in its snout that made a fine do-it-yourself fountain when you cupped a hand over its mouth. There was an ancient green boathouse at the park where you could buy gum and candy bars; and on Sundays there was a popcorn wagon. Above all, there was in this park a magnificent array of clanking, shining playground equipment.

Undisputed queen of the park was the tall and truly perilous slide. It stood, its proud head in the trees, blandly gazing over the water, whose flashing expanse was rivaled by the splendid blaze of the slide's swooping curves. It was so high that little kids had to be accompanied up the ladder and held on a lap going down, or hugged close to your side. This slide was usually very slick, especially after it had been well greased by putting wax paper on the seat of your pants. So high and smooth were its several curves that you could shoot off into the grass several feet. Also, the bottom was abrupt and, toward the end of the summer, inclined to be sharp from all the wear. Some kid was always cracking his head on it and being hauled off bloodily to be mended.

People didn't seem to be too concerned about accidents. I recall no accident-prevention campaigns, no first-aid courses, no safety drives. Life was comparatively simple, and though there were hazards—the lake, where on rare and signal occasions, somebody drowned—the possibility of injury in the park or on the contraptions we were always building in our own backyard was taken in stride. If you went swimming when you weren't supposed to, or ventured out too far, you got a licking and couldn't go in again for a week. If you got hurt, a mother simply tore up an old bed sheet, mopped the blood away, and applied iodine. Only the most impressive cases merited the attention of a doctor.

While suitably awed by this slide's occasional victims,

we weren't deterred. If anything, they only enhanced our enthusiasm and added to our sense of something daring and proprietary about that soaring structure.

We were especially jealous and bossy of it on Sunday afternoons. The town band would be snorting and thumping away on "The Stars and Stripes Forever" or "Pomp and Circumstance," boats dotted the lake, bathers swarmed the docks, and at the x-legged tables in the park people from farms and neighboring towns would be having picnics and family reunions. Kids, thick as the flies that hovered over their potato salad, would be lined up at "our" slide. We always felt vastly superior to these interlopers, and attempted to discourage them by lying about how many people fainted when they reached the top or had been seriously damaged on descending. And when our turn came, pride dictated that we try to impress them by going down headfirst or backward or by holding up the whole procession by rescaling the steep and slippery slopes on foot.

The chain swings were also both perilous and popular. They too seemed to us gallows-tall. If you were a good pumper, or had a good strong pumping partner, there would be a sudden thrilling buckle and jerk as you soared skyward. This everybody interpreted as warning that you were on the very verge of "going over." To actually "go over" the top bar was rumored to be a thrilling, appalling, and heroic disaster. Kids were always claiming they had "gone over," but we knew better, if only because they survived unmaimed. I never knew personally anyone who had met this mysterious and grimly enticing fate, but the legends abounded.

And again on Sunday afternoons we attempted to scare off the country kids by describing the supposed horrors of the chain swings. They didn't scare easy, however. Actually, due to a liberal exposure to haymows and windmills, they were tougher and braver than we were.

Also, once firmly ensconced in a swing, a child was king. Nothing short of an earthquake (or a parental summons) could force him to abdicate if he didn't want to. When we encountered one of these stubborn characters the best we could do was hurl taunts from the more humble nearby teeter-totters, proving our scorn for the compromise by the fury with which we banged and bounced them, or walked their slanting boards.

Later, dazzling additions were made to the attractions in the park. A broad wooden merry-go-round, for one, and some chains and handgrips affixed to a pole, called a "Giant Stride." At first, these two were very much in demand because of their uniqueness. We were proud of them; we tried to assume supreme command of them; we owned them. Yet for actual enjoyment nothing ever equaled the perennial challenge of these long clanking swings or the precarious splendors of that slide.

You didn't really have to go to the park, however—not if you had a good imagination and a big yard. A seesaw was such a simple thing to devise. All you needed was a sawhorse and a plank, and you were in business. True, it was not so finely balanced as those in the park; the sawhorse might tip over, and the board would skid from side to side. Nonetheless, it was fun, especially for younger children, chanting "Seesaw, Margery Daw" or making up their own rhymes. And when you were tired of this skidding and jouncing, you could use the board for a short, blunt (if not very satisfactory) slide.

If you were lucky enough to have an old barn or shed on the premises, as we were, with a second-story window, you could fashion a most imposing slide. One that could match most of the perils of the one in the park, with some splinters thrown in besides. You lugged to the shed the longest, smoothest plank you could find and propped one end in the opening. While two cronies steadied the other end from below, you mounted the steep wooden ladder inside.

The shed had the rusty, dusty, leather smell of an old buggy declining there, and an odor of the chickens that once had roosted among its side-curtains. The wooden rungs of the ladder were rough to the fingers, yet soft too, bleached with age. The top one was missing, so that if your legs were short somebody had to boost you into the opening.

When you poked your head through the blue rectangle, the ground seemed impossibly far away. An occasional coward would back right down again. One day a girl named Edith, of husky constitution but delicate stomach, just sat there whimpering for an hour. Despite taunts, exhortations, or the kindliest reasonings, she refused to budge in either direction.

Stern measures finally had to be taken; while the slide remained a novelty, we were cashing in on it by charging two cents a trip. The boys were forced to haul the board away and the rest of us agreed to leave her to get down as best she could. Some traitor went for her mother, who came charging over, mad at the whole bunch; worse, after losing all that business, we had to give her back her two cents.

For most of us, sheer honor demanded that we descend the slide, no-hands like some of the boys, or hanging on for grim death. No amount of fervent rubbing with soap or bread wrappers ever gave it the slickness and speed we

desired—and a good thing too. Yet we convinced ourselves
that we had created a rival to equal or possibly surpass
that reigning monarch of the park.

The genuine, most permanent attraction of every yard
worthy of the name was the swing. Even childless homes
usually had a swing of some kind. The status symbol of
the era, particularly for elderly, genteel people, was a
wooden affair with two seats face-to-face which glided
back and forth on a little slatted platform. To visit a home
so richly endowed was bliss. The children made a beeline
for the contraption, fought over turns to be conductor,
and transformed it instantly into a streetcar or a train.

For steady, day-to-day comfort and pleasure, though,
the best swing of all was the old-fashioned rope kind in
your own backyard. It occupied a unique and special
place in the life of a child—half person, half thing. A swing
could be shared—pushing or being pushed, or pumping.
But a swing could be used alone. A swing was like a faithful friend waiting for you when there was nobody else to
play with: You could wind up in it and feel the world
spin . . . lean over its seat on your tummy and watch the
lazily gliding ground . . . climb onto it, and grasping its
hairy hands with your own, propel yourself into a leafy,
dancing space.

You were king in a swing; it was your royal chariot,
your soaring throne. The ropes creaked and sighed companionably to your swooping, and the joints of the old
maple tree joined the secret conversation.

You took the swing's presence for granted. And when
something happened to it, when the seat broke, or the
rope frayed away, or you rushed out after a rain to find that
it had shrunk foolishly high, you felt a sense of shock and
loss. Almost a sense of betrayal. There was a loneliness

about it, akin to that when your mother was sick or gone.

It was unthinkable not to have such a swing. And when the old one wore out, or was about to, your father brought a thick yellow coil of new rope home from the hardware store and set about replacing it. Or your grandpa did. Our Grandpa Griffith prided himself on making the seat. Curly shavings piled up as he lovingly whittled and planed and carved, and with his big, bonehandled jack-knife notched the middle.

Then while an admiring audience gathered, Dad would shinny up the tree, bits of bark raining down. He would scramble out onto the limb to test its strength. Thump, the old rope would fall in a serpentine twining, and we would snatch it up and prance about with it.

Catching the new one from below, Dad would make lovely golden loops, baring and gritting his teeth as he knotted them securely, in a way that we always associated with intense endeavor on his part. We all thought him re-markably brave and strong, and watched his maneuvers as awed as if he were a mountain climber or one of the "human flies" shown sometimes on the newsreels at the movies. The climax would come when he sailed out on the rope and dangled for a minute, then slid down it fireman-style.

Everybody must try out the new swing, including Mother, who daintily crossed her ankles and shrieked and clutched at her skirts when Dad or some of the boys pushed her too high. Her petticoats rustled and laughed like the leaves; her white teeth flashed in the gathering dusk. For a few startled minutes she was not your mother but a capricious girl, and you didn't know whether to be pleased or upset.

Then breathless and brushing at her hair, she went

in to finish the dishes, while the children rushed to claim
the swing, fighting for turns, pumping singly or by twos.
A new swing always seemed to be filled with such joy and
vigor and power; its muscles distended, it squealed and
seemed to go higher. (Or were we only always getting
older and stronger to make its newness match our will?)
A pair of good pumpers could send it whipping into the
branches, almost into the stars. And like the chain swings
in the park, it too would buckle as if threatening to hurl
you over some mysterious pinnacle of fear and delight.

A swing could aid you socially . . . always a popular
gathering place. The most popular swing of all, especially
with the boys, was the bag swing. A bag swing had a
dash, a quality of recklessness lacking in dumb, staid tire
swings or the conventional two-roper. A lot of commotion always accompanied a bag swing, and usually its days
were numbered. Under the enthusiastic impact of lunging
bodies, the bag was always bursting open, or the rope
would break under the strain.

To make a bag swing you stuffed a gunny sack (tow
sack, some Southern neighbors called it) with straw and
tied it to a single rope which you then attached to the
arm of a tall and sturdy tree. With a running leap, you
straddled the bag and swung. A bag swing lent itself
marvelously to acrobatics. You could shinny up the rope
and entangle your feet in it and hang. You could dip
groundward, trailing an elegant hand while unseen audi-
ences applauded and unseen bands played.

To add to its drama we would set up a stepladder
beside the tree. Mounting the stepladder with the nimble
grace of circus acrobats ascending to their platforms, we
could catch the swing as it was tossed to us several times
by a cohort. Then, still under the delusion that we were

star performers intent on perfect timing, when the moment was right we would swing out on this bulky flying trapeze. Or sometimes we were equestrians and the swing was a galloping horse onto which we plunged.

Often a pal would follow you up the ladder and leap on top as you soared back. We used two stepladders when we could get them, one at each end of the arc; and there was much grunting and shrieking and shouting as kids piled on until somebody fell off, or the sack exploded, or the tree limb itself gave up with a shrill warning crack. Then down you all would thump onto the hard, bare ground, an ignominious conclusion to the dazzling act.

Somebody always got the wind knocked out of him, or got a black eye, or got mad, and mothers would come scolding out of houses to drag their dirty kids home. And for a few days, until somebody else put up a new swing, a kind of desolation set in. For summer had lost its luster, and life was scarcely worth living without that stellar attraction, a favorite swing. . . .

I'm sure playground sets serve their purpose. They spare dads all sorts of bother, and mothers all sorts of alarm. Besides, with so many women working, where would you find the mothers to worry about the children, anyway? With so many fathers traveling, or staying late at the office, or meeting customers at the club, where would you find the dads to scale the heights of a maple tree, rope in hand? Where would you find the old-fashioned grandpas with jackknives ready to whittle and carve? For that matter, where would you find the children—so often off at Scouts or camp or junior cotillion or the supervised playground?

As for the playground—the people who design its

equipment try to think of everything. They provide cement steps to climb on, cement culverts to crawl through. Not content with merely model streetcars, trains, and planes, they sometimes even drag a real one in.

On a recent trip to my childhood haunts, I found several of these marvels among the time-honored offerings in the park. But thank goodness the ancient clanking swings remain—swings tall enough to "go over." For it is these the kids still clamor to use. And though the safety committee got busy on the slide, it still muses grandly over the water, as the youngsters line up before it.

Somehow you just can't improve on a swing or a slide. They stand like monuments to the days when play was intense and wild and wonderful. When every house had a swing. When imagination meant more than money, and any child with a yard, a length of rope, a board, a tree, could be an acrobat . . . an equestrian . . . a king!

VIII

Washday at Dawn, Clothes on the Line

Don't get me wrong, I would be a woman bereft without my automatic washer; I love and applaud the matching yellow dryer standing smartly by its side. Hooray, I say, for spray starch and steam irons and mangles; and even louder hosannas for wash-and-wear fabrics that are rapidly making even that late unlamented job known as ironing almost obsolete.

I'm glad I don't have to roll out at the crack of dawn on washday and wind up with red, wrinkled hands and an aching back at night. Or slave all day beside a hot range shoving those heavy tugboats, flatirons, across corset covers and starched white shirts. And yet I sometimes miss the sheer commotion, mess, and drama of doing the laundry in the good old days.

The modern ease and convenience of our automated lives have taken something besides drudgery out of the domestic scene. Many tender side benefits and compensations, peculiarly female. For one thing, women have been robbed of the unspoken Monday morning competition that used to exist, at least in most small towns.

The truly ambitious housewife would struggle out of bed before daylight in the fervent hope of being the first to have her clothes on the line. Oh, those flapping banners, proudly proclaiming a woman's zeal! In our neighborhood everybody finally gave up trying to beat Mrs. Mansky, whose lines were always snapping and taunting their triumph by dawn. But the others—those who valued their standing at least—got in there and fought it out to be second. True, there were a few sluggards (my mother, for one) who refused to compete, and sometimes didn't have the evidence of their efforts out till after ten, or sometimes noon. Who sometimes even—imagine!—chose to wash on another *day*. But such rugged individuals were the exception.

The only times Mrs. Mansky didn't win the contest were when she was away visiting her daughter in Cherokee, or too sick to stagger forth with the bulging baskets at all. Everybody was so programmed to starting the week with Mrs. Mansky's washing that when her lines were vacant there was an uneasiness in the air. And although some women gloated, privately they were distressed. Once, when she was in the hospital six weeks with a broken hip, they couldn't stand it; they took turns going to her house and doing her wash. What's more, they saw to it that the Monday morning sunrise continued to do honor to her good name.

The whiteness of the clothes was another status symbol. No hucksters were needed to rouse our mothers with a feverish pitch about "ring around the collar" and "tattle-tale gray." They were in there pitching themselves, with strong yellow soap shaved into a scalding wash boiler, and a scrub board on which to bloody the knuckles if necessary to be sure that the dishtowels and the shirts and the long winter woolens came clean.

Some women made their own soap, out of hoarded fat drippings, water, and lye. A day's work in itself. Mother tried it only a couple of times, then balked and went back to Fels Naphtha. The soap was chopped up the night before. In fact, the whole works started then with the sorting of the clothes—strictly segregated: white, colored, dark—in separate piles, with the dirtiest put separately to soak. There was a great clanking of buckets and tubs and sloshing of water as Dad or a brother pumped and hauled, while one of us butchered the soap. The big oblong copper boiler would also be filled and put on the back of the stove to heat all night.

By morning it would be seething and stewing, ready for the whites which would be poked in and stirred about with a stick. An ex-broomstick kept for the purpose, smooth and sturdy and bleached with age. Fitting the boiler lid firmly on was like helmeting a querulous old armored king. He grumbled and sputtered. The teakettle chuffed its white whiskers to keep him company, the oatmeal bubbled in the pan. The blue granite coffeepot got into the act by boiling over—little brown beads joined the white ones scooting and hissing across the rosy lids of the range.

It was like having breakfast at the canning factory! Especially since by now someone was jerking the handle of the wooden washer back and forth.

In the days when I was very small, it was entirely a manual operation, including the hand-cranked wringer, which was clamped first to the machine, then to the rinsing tubs. From time to time Mother would stir the boiling clothes, bloated and puffy like an artist's drawing of the cheeks of the wind, or lift them, steaming and dripping, and flop them into the machine.

The tubs of rinse water waited on a bench, icy cold to your plunging arms. Mother sometimes let us pour in the bluing from the bottle, and participate in the magical upflooding of color—midnight blue at the bottom, diminishing to sheer cornflower blue when stirred about. How strange that it could make the clothes brighter.

All this equipment was kept on a latticed back porch which was covered by the purple and white discs of morning glories in summer, and in winter thickly roofed with snow. A cozy shelter in which to play, and a kind of treasure trove of possibilities. Unlike a lot of parents, ours didn't seem to mind when we appropriated the washday gear for whatever games our imaginations invented. The boiler lid made a marvelous shield for battles, the stick a goodly weapon. The boiler, dented and tarnished green-gold with age, was great for hauling each other bumpily about and riding down icy hills. And so were the round silvery tubs. We filled them with water and sailed little boats in them, and took our dolls swimming.

The clothes basket became a bassinet, a hammock in which to swing each other, a tepee, or a huge jungle hat. The machine itself was a fine hiding place, or we "drove it" across deserts, mountains, lakes, and into the very sky.

With the advent of an electric machine, kept properly in the basement of the newer, better house, washday was less hectic if only a little less dramatic. Mother still boiled her whites and blued her rinses. But now, thrillingly, all you had to do was stuff the clothes into the regal monster and listen to it churn them about. It sang as if it really enjoyed the job—*hummm-thug-thug, hummmm-thug-thug!* And the rubber rollers greedily gulped your offering and thrust them through flat and barely dripping. Look out, though, their hunger was almost frightening—don't let them grab a hand.

Old machine or new, Mother cheerfully resisted joining the race to the line. "Let them break their necks if they want to, I'll get mine out when I good and please." But she more than compensated by the pride she took in the ultimate display. "It's funny," she would mumble around the wooden pins in her mouth, "but I really *like* to hang out the clothes!" And no artist arranging his paintings did so with more care than that with which she riveted her products to the line. Sheets neatly doubled, bottoms up so that the breeze could blow them dry. And no helter-skelter arrangements either: all sheets marching together, all pillowcases on parade, then the rest of the aristocratic whites, which got priority in the water. After that the coloreds, each carefully with his kind, so that the rows of shirts or dresses dancing were like a chain of paper dolls.

She even made sure the colors didn't clash—no reds next to pinks—and entertained herself by hanging harmonious shades side by side.

"Slovenly" she dubbed anyone who bunched things carelessly together or tossed them pinless on a line. And rags or worn unmentionables were discreetly dried inside. "A woman is judged by her washing," she declared. And she was right. For people walked more then and had time to study not only your curtains and your flower beds but your clotheslines as they strolled by.

Sometimes, at our imploring, she reversed the sheets so that we might dive and fumble between their damply flapping sides. Or, washing and airing blankets, she would help us peg them into the ground for tents. We would creep in on all fours and sometimes camp all day, setting

up housekeeping with tea sets and dolls and limp bouquets
of dandelions. How secret and snug it was, hot and fragrant
with sun and grassy earth. While outside you could hear
the sheets and towels snapping as your mother visited with
a neighbor across the fence.

It was fun to help take the dry things down; they
collapsed with such sweetness against your face to be
folded and tucked into the creaking basket. The whites
were sometimes so dazzling they hurt the eyes.

Even in winter Mother, bundled up to the eyebrows,
battled snow and wind to hang her clothes outside. Stocking cap, scarf, an old overcoat of Dad's, even gloves with
the fingertips cut out. Not so much to dry them as to give
them the quick freeze that's an even more effective bleach-
ing agent than the sun. Dresses, trousers, underwear—
everything soon became stiff and flat as cardboard dum-
mies. You could stack them against a wall and they
wouldn't fall down. In the end you hauled them back in,
to the rack that had been set up over the hot-air register,
and bent them, crackling, over its bars. As they began to
wilt they gave off a steamy scent that mingled pleasantly
with the smell of supper cooking.

Food on washday always seemed festive, somehow. A
kind of appeasement because of the commotion and the
work and everybody being so tired. Noon dinner was in-
variably "slumgullion," an enormous beef vegetable stew,
which included all the leftovers in the icebox, and was
heavy on onions and tomatoes. For some reason we loved
it, maybe because Mother made it seem a special treat.
Supper was always beefsteak. Floured, pounded, and
thoroughly fried. With chocolate cake and peaches for
dessert. Mother or one of us managed to stir up the cake
and get it in the oven, and its rich promise wafting across

the premises helped to cancel out the soapy laundry smell.

Really zealous housewives often did their ironing as well on washday. Some were even known to boast, "I washed, ironed, cleaned, and baked bread today." Such gluttons for punishment were anathema to my mother, whose energy quotient was low. Also, she considered other things more important. "Women were not meant to be workhorses," she would insist, gratefully pulling the plug for the machine to drain, and shaking the teakettle to see if there was enough hot water to warm her sponge bath.

Though the heavens (and clotheslines) fall, as they sometimes did, it was her inflexible habit to bathe, change, unwind her kid curlers, cream her hands, and take a nap before our father got home. Thus, however huge the day's undertaking, it always concluded with a rested, powdered, pretty mother whose back might be aching, but whose femininity was intact.

After supper, full of good intentions, she would let us help her dampen the clothes. This too she rather enjoyed, the whisking water bottle, or the shake of dripping fingers, and then rolling things smoothly up into little bundles. Cuddled into the clothes basket they looked like loaves of bread dough set to rise. She might even boil up a batch of starch. But it took her a day or two to recuperate from the washing; she seldom could bring herself to tackle the ironing the *next* day, which was the traditional time.

"And the longer I put it off the more I dread it," she scolded herself. "If I could only make myself get *at* it."

A little flock of flatirons, boat-shaped, faintly pink, stood permanently in drydock on the back of the kitchen stove. They were generally warm enough for pressing anything you needed in a hurry. The curved wooden handle which clamped onto them was kept on a shelf in the warming oven. The board, fatly padded with table felt and swaddled in old sheets, leaned companionably nearby, its scorched and mottled skin resembling that of a Shetland pony. When it got too brown and brittle Mother would simply unpin and unpeel a few layers.

On the day when Mother finally put down her eternal reading and forced herself officially to iron, it was essential that a fiercely hot fire be built in the stove. A good shaking down of the ashes. Plenty of cobs and kindling crackling. Coal buckets well filled. All this before the "menfolk" departed for jobs or school. Soon the cheeks of the stove would be apple-red. The irons, shoved forward, would sizzle to the touch of a moistened finger, and she would begin, starting with the shirts to get them over with.

What did women think about as they ironed in those days, I wonder? Before radios and television sets to entertain them with music and soap operas and quiz shows. I have no idea, but I do know my mother whistled and sang. Despite her hand-wringing procrastination, she seemed to take pleasure in the deed, once begun. Coming in after school, we would hear the cheery notes above the click-click-click of the gliding iron.

The house would smell toasty from the hot clean cloth, and again she would have something baking, drop cookies maybe or gingerbread, so as not to waste the oven. She would look up and smile, her gold tooth flashing, and gesture with a kind of proud surprise at her handiwork. The neat stacks of pure white linens, the shirts and dresses blossoming from the backs of chairs.

"I saved the napkins and handkerchiefs for you. You can do them after you've put some more coal on the fire for me, honey, and hung your own things away. I'm just about worn out." She would sigh, but her eyes would be shining. "Just look what I've accomplished!"

Look what I've accomplished.

Hard labor though the laundry was, a woman was repaid by her sense of personal value. With loving hands and arms and back she kept her family clean. Her clotheslines were her banner, proudly flown . . .

I wouldn't want to trade places with her—no. I'm grateful that my equipment is as attractive as our stereo, and sounds almost as pleasant; that washday is any old time you feel like tossing something in. I'm glad I don't have to get my fingers frostbitten hanging things out in winter, or in summer watch the skies worriedly for rain. But I sometimes get a little homesick for women's voices calling to each other around the clothespins in their mouths, and the fragrance of sun-sweet garments that have danced all day outdoors.

And I recall, with a little pang, the flower-garden look of the kitchen as Mother ironed, and her expression of sheer womanly achievement, taking tender inventory.

IX

Carry Me Back to the Farm

For children raised in city or suburbs there is nothing more fascinating than a farm. The elementary school my youngsters attended staged an annual pilgrimage for the sole purpose of letting pupils hear cows moo and pigs grunt, pet sheep, hold baby ducklings, and see chickens live and clucking about instead of prone in a supermarket. And many farmers do a nice seasonal business by taking on a few kids or even whole families for an old-fashioned summer vacation on a farm.

Farms were a part of my childhood's landscape, a way of life in our town. Farms flowed all about us and right down to the lake on the opposite shores. Five minutes from Main Street you were flanked by fields and pastures, vast loamy acres that were black with plowing in spring and fall, shimmering green and gold all summer, with windmills rising like slender chrysanthemums against the open sky.

In Storm Lake itself tall red grain elevators reared beside the railroad tracks, along with storage bins and cattle sheds and pens and ramps for loading stock. In the night long freights lumbered through, drawing their loads of cattle or hogs to market. Often they halted and switched and backed, in a clattering, squealing cacophony of couplings, along with the squealing and bawling of the doomed creatures, who sometimes stuck their noses through the slats. A strong, sharp barnyard aroma drifted out to blend with the resiny smell of the lumberyards. Finally a brakeman's lantern would cut a fiery arc, the whistle hooted, and with a painful screeching, as if it were in mortal torment, the train would gather itself for the journey ahead.

Walking home after the movies you would often be held up by these proceedings; and they would wake you, mournful and yet vaguely exciting in the night.

Practically all our relatives lived on farms, and both my parents had been born in the country. Mother's parents moved to town when she was a little girl so she felt she had escaped what was to her, for some reason, an appalling fate. She loathed and detested farms. The most miserable year of her life, she claimed, was the one when Dad, full of ebullient hopes, had persuaded her to "go on the farm." "It rained every day and ruined the corn and we lost everything we had," she claimed. Mother wept almost as copiously as the skies. At last, hopes drenched, they moved back to town.

Most of my father's life he served farmers in some capacity, selling them cream separators or incubators or tractors, bargaining with their wives for chickens, or managing Vic Sjostrom's big poultry house. Nonetheless we felt vastly superior to country kids, including our numerous cousins. This did not diminish our delight in going to visit them, where we pretended a pretty ignorance of rural ways, and it pleased us no end that they resented us and called us names like "Stuck up" and "City slickers."

Our favorite cousins to visit were the Pattens, distant relatives on Mother's side. Old Tom, as we called him, owned half the county but he enjoyed playing the curmudgeon, resisting cars and gravel roads, scolding, "People oughta stay home where they belong." Three sons were still on the farm when we spent our summer vacations among them, and they seemed to us truly giants upon their earth, in fearless command of windmills and threshing machines and monstrous plodding horses. Their hair was almost as red as the weathered barns, their eyes the pure blue of their overalls, their skin the rusty-bronze color of the bays. Oak-tall they were, and when you beat futilely against them with your fists their muscles were oak-hard. They teased us unmercifully and always won at carom, which was no fair since their enormous knuckles were so skilled and strong. And they would put on boxing gloves and spar around with us, letting us poke happily at them, and then let us have it! Sometimes so hard we got a nosebleed and ran yelling to their mother.

They were always playing tricks on us.

Once, in great elation, my sister caught a tiny field mouse which she named Gwendolyn, for herself, and bedded down in a matchbox, despite Cousin Allan's warning, "You better watch out. Mice bite, and they grow fast. Are you sure you want to keep it in your room?" Oh, yes, yes, she exclaimed, she wasn't a bit afraid, it was such a teensy-weensy mouse.

But that night those wretched Goliaths crept into the room and spirited off her baby. In its place they substituted a fat, full-grown dowager of a mouse which they'd just caught in the pantry. And they were lurking in the doorway the next morning when she leaped out of bed and raced eagerly to the dresser to open Gwendolyn's bassinette. Roaring with laughter they watched the mouse jump out and the girl run screaming. "See?" they gloated. "We told you mice grow fast!"

They rigged up a giant swing for us in the maple tree and pushed us to terrifying heights. They taught us to milk, or tried to, laughing at our tipsy perch on the one-legged stool, our feeble efforts to squeeze a drop or two from the dusty leather teats. (How merrily the pail rang when they took over, how the warm foam rose!) They amused us by sending jets of milk toward the mouths of the hovering cats.

They boosted us up into the haymow and patiently came after us when we were scared to come down. They let us climb the silver scaffolding of the windmill. Our brother climbed fearlessly to the very wheel sometimes and touched its magical blades. I never got beyond the first platform. It trembled and swayed slightly, as if in gentle warning. Above, its mystical head seemed to be looking left and right, a genteel pompadoured lady with a comb in her hair, visiting with the wind and watching for something in the sky. That this elegant personage provided the power to suck up water from the well and bring it into great moss-grown tanks and troughs where thirsty stock drank only added to the marvel.

We gathered eggs for Cousin Louie, setting forth with baskets, to hunt them in nests and mangers, a veritable Easter morning every day. Sometimes the fragile globes were newlaid and still warm. We were warned to stay clear of the setting hens—their yellow beaks would stab if you tried to disturb their precious clutch. We walked gingerly, carrying this rare cargo, perhaps unconsciously recognizing its worth. For every farm wife was expected to raise chickens, and the egg money was usually consid-

ered hers (in that way she often had more financial inde-
pendence than her sisters in town). In some households
she was even allowed to keep the butter money. A cream
separator stood in every pantry; hers the job of operating
this contraption, and cleaning it, and churning the butter,
most of which was carried to town and sold along with
the eggs on Saturday.

Each morning we also ran or sauntered a half mile
down the road to get the mail. Grasshoppers, jewel-green,
dropped like bullets in the ruts at our bare feet, butterflies
twinkled, red- or gold-winged blackbirds flocked in the
pastures. From barbed-wire fences meadowlarks sang.
Along the road telephone wires hummed. You could hear
them clearly if you pressed your ears against the hot
wooden poles. It was like listening to distant voices in
mysterious conversation, as if the very poles were humming and throbbing to the secret words people were saying
to each other.

There was something melancholy and yet reassuring
about it; the country could be so lonely. In a farmhouse
the incessant ringing of the telephone both relieved and
yet somehow enhanced the loneliness. You kept listening
for your own ring, or the ring of neighbors on your party
line, and if the loneliness got too bad you could "rubber."
This meant carefully picking up the receiver and listening
in. Sometimes people got so interested they forgot and
butted into the conversation.

The mailboxes were clustered at the crossroads, looking like flat-headed dwarfs, many of them with their
mouths open as if hungry, begging, "Feed me!" We would
squat in the chirping, sun-sweet grasses, braiding clover
and watching for the cloud of dust that signaled the approach of the mailman's Model T. He would pull up at

last and stuff the gaping mouths until tomorrow—with yesterday's newspapers and *Capper's Farmer* and letters from married children also farming, most of them, at Sac City or Rembrandt or Eagle Grove.

The men, in the fields since daybreak or before, would be hungry by ten o'clock, and we'd take another hike with their midmorning lunch. Syrup pails crammed with thick pork sandwiches, hardboiled eggs, wedges of pie or cake, along with Mason jars filled with cold coffee or lemonade. No ice, no thermos jugs. Our cousins *whoaed* their teams, took off their sweaty straw hats, wiped their streaming faces on red or blue bandanas, and quaffed and gulped with gusto. Then back to cultivating the corn, or cutting the golden oats or the bright green alfalfa, while we wandered the pasture, waded in the cold clear waters of the creek, caught crawdaddies, or resumed our play in a shady grove or one of the marvelous assortment of buildings that constituted a farm.

The farm stretched farther than the eye could follow. And at its corner was assembled a veritable village of buildings—practically every one of them bigger than the cramped cottage that housed the family. The long pig-house with its squealing, grunting, dozing, rooting occupants who spilled over into the rutted lot, there to wallow in muddy spills or trip about, curly tails jaunty, and strangely dainty on their cleft high heels. The musky-smelling cowshed where the heavy-uddered creatures were relieved of their burden morning and night. The brooder house and chickenhouse, smelling of feathers and chicken dirt and lime. In addition there were the corncribs, the machine sheds, the silos and granary, and an immense red barn.

All this to be explored, hidden in, played in, while in

adjacent dusky groves and fragrant humming weedy lots could be found an assortment of abandoned buggies, corn-planters, harrows, discs and other machines worthy of an amusement park.

The barn was our favorite place, however, and we usually saved it for afternoon. The barn was like the castle on the grounds, its haymow surely the place where Rum-pelstiltskin spun flax into gold. Anyway, here the straw and hay were piled, great fluffy drifts of it, a veritable sea in which to wallow. Bales of hay were stacked to the rafters, and these we arranged into steps and platforms to leap from. There was also a long rope tied to an overhead beam, with a metal hook at its end. By grasping this and kicking off we could soar almost out the open haydoor that framed the sky, before dropping. The hay was sweet and dusty and tickling. Swallows darted in and out, pigeons strutted, crooning. Below, we could hear a few horses in their stalls, while outside, from the shimmering meadows came the plaintive, lonely call of mourning doves.

Finally, when we were done with jumping and swing-ing and screeching hayfights, we would climb on the broad wooden gates to the pasture and watch for the men coming in from the fields. With a glad shout we'd run to meet them, begging for a ride. Grinning good-naturedly, they would boost us onto the broad slippery backs. The horses had a rank-sweet vinegary odor; we clung to their dry brittle manes or a knob of the jingling harness while our cousins led the beasts to the watering tank, where they bent their heads to drink great noisy slobbering draughts of the bitter-cold water. Then plonk-plonk-plonk up to the barn and through its half-open divided doors. Their hooves struck out a kind of puddingy music on the bare

earth floors. The smell of manure and hay and horse and harness made the nostrils tingle.

Now the dreamy afternoon quality of the barn changed, came suddenly strongly alive. There was a brisk sound of buckets clanking, the whisking of pitchforks and hay, the rumble and rattle of ears of corn being dumped into the feeding bins. While over all would settle the rich and rhythmic harmonies of great teeth munching.

Even if we had already spent our allotted time on Patten's farm, we were always invited back for threshing. Partly to share in the heady drama of this major event of the summer, but also to help. Cooking for threshers must

be experienced to be believed. The very term has come
to signify something Paul Bunyanesque, gargantuan. A
thresher doesn't eat a mere serving of potatoes, he downs
the whole bowl; nor a piece of pie or cake—at least half
of it, sometimes all, plus maybe an entire jar of pears or
peaches. For a full week before the onslaught of threshers
every available hand was welcomed for the preparing of
fruits and vegetables, the cooking and baking.

My sister and I pitched in, along with an assortment
of married daughters who came home with fat milky
babies to be nursed and diapered and added to the gen-
eral atmosphere of urgency, confusion, and celebration.
For this was the first step of the harvest season. The corn,
"knee-high by the Fourth of July," now stood a tall green
rustling forest higher than a man's head. ("Don't go out
in it, kids, you could get lost.") It must await its hour of
picking and husking in the fall. But already there had
been two cuttings of alfalfa, and now the oats were ready.
Ripe in mid-July, they had been cut, the bundles dotting
the landscape like a candlewick spread. Then, as if Indians had come in the night, the bundles had been piled
into tepee-shaped shocks. Now all these little wigwams
were to be gathered and delivered of their precious grain.

The man who owned the threshing machine usually
came the night before. Excitedly we awaited the arrival
of that mighty dragon in the dusk. At last there came a
puffing and clanking down the road, a smell of smoke, a
glitter of sparks as the steam engine that hauled it turned
into the lane. Like a great leashed beast it followed, bigger
than a fire engine and more imposing, with its belts and
wheels and gears and platforms and mighty stacks.

"Now you kids be careful; stand back." My sister and
I didn't need to be cautioned, but our brother joined the

men, circling, spitting, exclaiming, as the behemoth was set up for the following day's performance down by the barn.

The teams and wagons and hayracks began arriving shortly after sunrise, driven by the men from five or six neighbor families who belonged to the threshing ring. The whole barnyard became a hubbub of activity that rivaled the circus in its lively, lusty noise. Harnesses jangled, wheels creaked, horses whinnied and sometimes reared, men's voices called and kidded and cussed. Oscar, the man who owned the machine, bald as a stone and sooty, had fired up and the boiler was going, puffing clouds of steam.

Empty hayracks rattled off to the fields and came back slowly, fat and groaning with their whiskery load. The machine, now primed and roaring for its task, was fed and began to spew out its separate products: straw in golden blasts, a sandy pile of chaff, while into the wagons flowed a steady silken river of the grain.

The wagons then were pulled into the open-ended granary; and there, under its pitched roof, the teams were maneuvered over the complex machinery of an elevator, which would carry their slippery cargo in buckets to be tipped into the bins. All this was horsepower in the purest sense. For outside, another team of horses plodded in patient circles merely to keep the shafts and gears and belts and chains in motion.

Our brother was privileged to be a part of all this, serving sometimes as grease monkey to the machine, sometimes wielding a pitchfork on the strawstack, or even driving a team. Mere females were confined to the kitchen. Cousin Louie, a strict Puritan, felt it was highly improper for girls of any age to hang around men, especially in pants. The fact that we were just banties, and our non-existent charms were practically swallowed in our brother's old Scout pants (discards, but we thought dashing) made no difference. On threshing day we wore skirts and could appear only with bowls of food or the big blue granite coffeepot in hand.

Everything had to be cooked and ready and on the enormous table with its checkered cloth by noon. Home-canned pork and beef swimming in gravy; fried chicken; four or five kinds of vegetables; mountains of potatoes; pickles, relishes, jelly; staggering bowls of coleslaw; hot biscuits and cornbread and thick slabs of white bread (some men made sandwiches of everything within reach); pie and cake and rice pudding, plus applesauce and peaches and berries and cherries. Everything crammed bowl by jar by jowl to save both time and room. (Nobody waited for courses or for each other.)

Outside, the ravenous men would have consulted the thick nickel watches in their overall bibs, and begun watering their horses and hanging the feedbags on their noses before the first shift headed toward the wash-house. There, itching with straw and grain, sweat-drenched (some of them wore long underwear winter or summer), they stood around awaiting their turn to wash from the chipped white basin set on a wooden bench. A pail of cistern water and a dipper stood beside it; nailed to the tree was a combination tin mirror, soap dish, and comb holder, and beside that a long red-bordered roller towel.

The threshers washed with abandon, plunging their faces and sometimes their heads into the basin, sloshing and spluttering, finally plastering down their hair and combing it with the big-toothed tin communal comb. Then, like great ruddy beasts to be fed, the first shift came clumping into the kitchen. The food disappeared with incredible speed into their seemingly bottomless pits and was replaced again and again. Full at last, they sauntered into the yard to josh and smoke and chew and spit while the second batch took its turn.

On threshing day women got dinner all morning and washed dishes and got supper all afternoon. But it was all lively and rich with talk and purpose, and somehow festive—the click and clatter of bone-handled knives and forks, and the heavy ironstone plates, brown-bordered with a fleur-de-lis in the center, most of them as checked and lined as the faces of the women who handled them.

Supper was more fun, like a party. Though some of the men had gone home to do their chores, others worked until dark. And when at last they trooped wearily into the lamplit kitchen, they often found their wives, who'd come bearing further food. More plates were squeezed onto the already crowded table, new offerings of baked beans or potato salad or coleslaw added. Children were shooed outside with their heaping plates, there to resume their madly chasing games, while inside their elders sat visiting. Bone-tired as everybody was, a sense of rejoicing and celebration prevailed. More coffee was poured, more pies were cut.

All that food! All that plenty! A sense of the overflowing bins and barns was in the air. A sense of reaping some vital harvest, not only of the crops but of human effort. Friends and neighbors linked together in a common triumph. The success of this day was the success of them all; and tomorrow it would be repeated down the road, and next week somewhere else. So the harvest didn't stop here, the harvest moved in a perpetual ring of helping and sharing.

And later, carrying our flickering kerosene lamps up

the steep back stairs, settling down into the fluffy feather beds, we could smell the sweetness of cut fields . . . hear the humming and chirping sounds of a summer night at the end of an epic day's labor. Everything seemed to be singing a lively little song of fulfillment and content. We didn't feel superior to country people anymore—we kind of envied them.

X

Mother's Apron

"Oh, Mother, buy an apron, please let's buy an apron!"
children always urge at church bazaars. Aprons have a
special fascination for them; they are forever tugging
mothers toward that table where other women swarm,
picking and choosing from among the bright displays: the
aprons dancing saucily overhead or piled in colorful heaps
upon the counter. Striped aprons, ruffled aprons, old-
fashioned checkered aprons trimmed with rickrack and
braid and appliqué. Smart modern ones of orange burlap,
hand-painted with abstract designs. A froth of cocktail
whimsies of impractical, unwashable net, all bead- and
sequin-trimmed.

And suddenly, though an apron's the last thing you
want, a little fever of excitement touches you. You too
begin to root through this female flower garden and pluck
a bright bouquet.

I sometimes wonder why aprons are still so popular
when so few of us actually have much use for them any
more? Now, there was a good excuse for aprons in our
mothers' day. In that blissful pre-cholesterol era hardly

anybody broiled or pressure-cooked; no, foods were fried lengthily, smokily, often sputteringly, in good old-fashioned lard.

To bake a cake you didn't simply open a package and make a few absentminded gestures with an electric mixer. You coped long and lovingly with flour and eggs and maybe clabbered milk, pausing for good measure to shake down the ashes in the old coal range, smash more kindling across your knees, and shovel in more cobs or chunks of rich, black, dusty coal. An apron was not only part of a woman's uniform of domesticity, it was protection.

But today, with our instant mixes and frozen foods, only the dedicated cook spends very much time in her easy-clean push-button kitchen. And even when she does, her usual costume is shorts or slacks. So who needs an apron?

What inspires us then to make and buy and bestow aprons upon each other, or to acquire them for ourselves? Is it that an apron is so . . . womanly? That apron strings are subtly entangled with childhood memories—the days

when mothers stayed home to sew and clean and cook and can. The days when a mother was always *there*.

Women dressed like women then, and anyone who didn't was considered either sinful or slightly cracked. Like a certain Mrs. Gottwald, a big, coarse woman who lived on the edge of our town and farmed along with her menfolks. We'd see her clumping along the street sometimes in boots and overalls and a bulky, ill-smelling jacket. (It was rumored she even chewed tobacco.)

Mrs. Gottwald was a far cry from the elegant temptress, Marlene Dietrich, who descended on America in trousers, but Marlene was even more shocking because she posed a threat. What if designers decreed that all women must give up that precious symbol of their sex, the skirt? They loved their petticoats and hand-embroidered corset covers! They had mass meetings about it in the basement of the library, and wrote letters of protest to the newspapers, and threatened to boycott the movies.

One woman was so anti-trousers that she even refused

to let her daughter wear gym bloomers; sent a note to school demanding that the teacher allow her to exercise in middy blouse and skirt, or else! I remember that our own mother was acutely distressed when my sister and I began borrowing our brothers' Boy Scout knickers for hikes. Girls' knickers had been introduced by then, but they were considered rather daring. Besides, we couldn't afford them, so we had to feel bold and adventurous and worry our mother by sauntering forth in the Boy Scout pants.

Meanwhile, mothers continued to prepare for their day's assault upon the premises by donning layer upon layer of garments, culminating with a "housedress." A "housedress" might be vaguely pretty, with a bow or a few buttons on it, but mostly it was plain, functional, and washable, with all elements of character or imagination reduced to the absolute minimum.

The costume was then crowned with a dustcap. The cap was often plain sturdy gingham to match the dress. Or it might be a perky concoction of lace and ribbon rosettes. In any case, it served the purpose of protecting the hair from the dust that mothers whacked or shook or swept from the house.

And always, as a kind of extra fortification from all this, a mother wore an apron. She put it on over her housedress in the morning, and she didn't remove it until she cleaned up for the afternoon. Then, like as not, she donned a fresh one from her ample stock.

Women were better organized then, perhaps because they had to be. They seldom had a car in the driveway to whisk them off to meetings or the supermarket while the clothes washed and dried. My mother certainly never did the impulse cleaning to which I'm prone, nor popped a

pie in the oven or started an ironing after dark. As with
her neighbors, each day was sacred to its appointed tasks
—the laundry, the baking, the scrubbing; what's more,
she rose early, accomplished the scheduled undertaking,
and was ready for the sacred rite of making herself pre-
sentable by two o'clock. (To be "caught dirty" any time
after three would have been sheer disgrace.)

This involved at least a sponge bath with a kettle of
cistern water heated on the stove, the neat doing-up of
hair with a number of pins and tortoiseshell combs, putting on a "good" dress as opposed to a housedress, and
silk instead of cotton stockings, finishing off with a touch
of rice powder and a dab of cologne. She was then ready
for any callers who might drop in; or she'd lie down with
the latest installment of a Kathleen Norris serial.

This brief span during the afternoon was the only
time she was minus an apron. And when she arose to start
supper, did she change, as we are wont to, into something
comfortable if sloppy? No, indeed, she simply protected
her daintiness with a nice fresh apron. Sometimes a big
apron that encircled her neck like loving arms; sometimes
one that tied at the waist in a bow that brothers or your
dad would yank when they wanted to tease her. If company was coming, it would be a fancy apron, all organdy
frills, the kind women still wear for serving dinners and
sociables at the church. But family apron or company
apron, it was always crisp and pretty and clean, and she
often wore it to the table.

Frequently she continued to wear it on into the evening after the dishes were done. Standing at the back
fence visiting with a neighbor, strolling about the yard
to see about her flowers, or sitting on the porch in the

twilight watching the children playing Redlight or catching fireflies in a jar. And if the air was chilly, she wrapped her arms in her apron to keep them warm.

An apron was a part of Mother—like her laugh or her eyes or her big black pocketbook. And it was more than her protection against the hazards of cooking and keeping house—it was a kind of protection for you as well. It was big enough to shelter you too sometimes if you were cold. There was always a handkerchief for you in one of its roomy pockets. It was a part of her lap.

And her apron gave you assurance. Rushing in from school or play, even if you didn't see or hear her, you felt better just finding that apron hanging behind the kitchen door or dangling across a chair. Her apron, smelling of cookies and starch and Mother. It comforted you. It made you feel secure. . . .

Sometimes I worry about us a little, we busy, often absent mothers in our slacks. What do we leave behind to greet the child when he comes seeking us? What consoling reminder of our presence?

Maybe that's why our youngsters instinctively want us to own aprons. Lots of aprons. And to wear one now and then. Why we ourselves can't resist buying them at bazaars. Maybe we still feel the strong, sweet tug of apron strings. We remember the time when an apron meant a lap to be cuddled on . . . a pocket with a hanky to wipe your nose on . . . Someone who cared about you. The days when a mother's apron symbolized love!

XI

The Mail-Order Catalog

"Look, children, see what's come in the mail," I summoned my young one day. "A big, fat mail-order catalog!"

They rushed up to see what I was so pleased about. And reacted with about as much enthusiasm as if I'd just presented them with a big, fat telephone directory. Its plethora of riches failed to impress them—they see all this and more in store windows every day. And who ever heard of sending away for something you haven't both seen and been fervently exhorted to buy on TV? Politely they listened to my promises that when the catalog got a little older I'd let them cut it up for paper dolls—and escaped.

Somewhat saddened, I stood sniffing its elusive, nostalgic scent of thin, inky pages, and thick, glossy ones. Letting myself be whisked back to the days when the arrival of mail-order catalogs signaled spring and fall. Like spying your first robin, or a scarlet maple leaf. *Sears and Roebuck. Montgomery Ward.* What magical words! For if you lived in a small town or the country, they brought the whole thrilling world to your door.

This was important in several ways. Snowbound much of the winter, without much choice in merchandise in the few available stores, these vast packages of print and pictures spread before dazzled eyes almost everything known to the needs of man. Entire families were often clothed and outfitted from their pages, from a baby's first diapers on through the wedding dress. Whole houses were furnished by mail—curtains, rugs, parlor suite, nickel-plated stove, and even the kitchen sink. But more, the catalog was a source of information, of contact, a glimpse of fabulous people at work and play. A springboard for hope, the touchstone of dreams.

To children, the arrival of a new catalog was as if Santa Claus himself had walked in the door. We fought over turns to explore it, lying enrapt on the floor. The tissue-thin pages rustled as you turned them, like the whisper of young leaves; the shiny colored ones held the vivid promise of rainbows. We spent hours poring over them, especially before Christmas, greedily drawing up long impossible lists from the section marked Toys. Desperately though we yearned, fervently though we believed in the miracle of possessing, I don't think it was the getting that really mattered. In these orgies of imagination we were fulfilled.

In the same way we spent thousands of nonexistent dollars fervently filling out blanks from old ones as we "ordered" the most expensive items—furniture, jewelry, furs.

Most important of all were the paper dolls. With the advent of a new catalog we were free to race for the scissors and start cutting up the old. Each of us having chosen a basic beauty, we would then whack off the heads and feet of other models in order to equip her with a wardrobe worthy of a queen. True, they were often in curious positions, and the garments didn't always fit; no matter, the dolls continued to beam and that was good enough for us.

Again, we would choose someone we wanted to be. Gloria Swanson, Aunt Tressa, the minister, the mayor, a town belle—and hunt until we found a fancied likeness. We then cut out families for them—dolls that suited and matched their real or imagined circles. My brother dubbed these, for some strange reason, our "Hippity People"— perhaps because of the way they danced across the floor in a breeze or a blast from the hot-air furnace. Each of us picked a corner of the dining room where we set up housekeeping with our chosen family.

They became vitally real to us one long, cold winter when we were housebound with a succession of measles, mumps, and chicken pox. Gloria Swanson visited back and forth with Uncle Henry, the minister, the judge's family. Their children went to parties and dances, had weddings, and when one of them got torn in two, had a funeral. (We found everything in the catalog but the casket.) Then one day when the snow was melting, my brother took the lot of them outside for a boatride. He was gone a long time. Returning, he confessed. The boat had upset and all our Hippity People were drowned. We all cried. Somehow, it spelled the end of our catalog paper dolls. And the beginning of our growing up.

Yet we never outgrew our awed admiration for the beautiful creatures in those books. What grace they had, standing hand on hip as they chatted with each other, what charm, what style. On them even a housedress looked enticing, while the men were so suave and handsome they glorified even a pair of Big Huck overalls. In the magic

land they inhabited there was no dirt, no dishwater, no floors to scrub, no spilled oatmeal. Everyone was young, radiant, and enchanting; and it seemed that if only you could obtain their garments for yourself or your parents, somehow your own dull, small, everyday world would become radiant and enchanting as well. How was it possible to believe otherwise, especially when you read the poetic prose in which they were described?

Though Mother too faithfully studied and loved her catalogs, she seldom sent away for things. "It's hard to tell how things really look from a picture," she said. "And besides you can't always be sure they'll fit. Also," she reasoned, "we should support our hometown merchants. They've been good to us." ("Good to us" meant letting us have credit when times were hard.) We found her attitude frustrating, in view of this surefire magic. She didn't have many clothes, and my sister and I longed desperately to send away and get her a dress.

A dress was simply beyond our means, even after weeks of saving, so we decided to settle for a hat. We picked out the prettiest we could find, not a very big hat, but one richly adorned with fruit and flowers. Eagerly we filled out the order blank, stealthily emptying our banks and slipping off to the post office to buy a money order. We could hardly wait. We wanted it in time for Easter. Our suspense was agonizing as the weeks slipped by. Every time she longingly fingered a hat downtown, or spoke about trimming an old one, we were tempted to tell her.

At last, a few days before Easter, the mail truck stopped before our house. As the driver marched up the walk and knocked we thought we would explode. "But we didn't order anything!" Mother protested, even as we began to shout: "Surprise! Surprise!" Baffled, she opened the box, lifted it out of the tissue paper, and there it was in all its glory. Even more gorgeous than we had imagined, rosy and shiny and velvet-ribboned, a veritable cornucopia of fruit and flowers.

"Oh, my!" Mother exclaimed, looking slightly dismayed. She picked it up gingerly, turning it around on her hand. "This is for *me*?" She'd never worn anything but the plainest hats; obviously she was almost too overcome with joy to speak.

She went at once to the mirror and put it on, with some difficulty, over her generous mounds of hair. Her hair was her crowning glory—she had the distinction of having the most in town. The hat sort of rode on the back of it like a ship precariously perched upon a wave. Until that moment it had never occurred to us that the hat might not become her. In our loving dreams she would be transformed before our eyes into a likeness of one of those dream-creatures of the catalog.

Instead, Mother turned to us looking stricken—half sad, half amused. "Oh, girls, girls, it's the most beautiful hat

in the world!" she cried, embracing us. "Just wait, I'll curl
my hair Saturday night and Sunday I'll have my powder
on. It'll look just—fine!"

It did. It almost did. We all complimented her vastly
when she was ready for church, and so did her friends
when she got there. But something was wrong and we
knew it, with a queer wrench in the region of our stom-
achs. It was our first troubled sip of that wry brew, dis-
illusionment. I think we grew up a little that day, as we
had on the death of our paper dolls.

Mother loyally wore the hat—how long I don't recall.
After a while it didn't look funny on her any more, it
simply became a part of her, like her dependable blue
crepe dress. When its flowers began to wilt, its fruit to
wither, she even doctored them up and wore it some more.

She was actually regretful when at last she was forced to abandon it. "I'll never forget this hat," she said, and she spoke for all of us. . . .

I think of it now on that rare occasion when a catalog comes in the mail. (You have to signify your need and desire to obtain a catalog if you live in the city, and order something now and then to be kept on the mailing list.) I thought of it as I tried to rouse in my children the sense of delight that a catalog used to bring. But a catalog cannot be the passport to wonder to them that it was to us. These children who are so rich in material things are desperately poor in the need for make-believe.

No, really to thrill to the magic of a catalog you must live in the country or a little town. And be a pigtailed dreamer in the days when winters were long and lonely . . . and paper dolls came alive . . . and a hat was truly a Hat to be worn lengthily, head high, by a mother who loved her little girls.

XII

Whatever Happened to Silence and Singing?

Whatever happened to silence? The silence that lets you hear crickets chirring in the grass, birds in leafy branches, or just the rhythmic music of your own thoughts? For that matter, what's happened to singing—the kind that once spilled joyously out of everyday human throats? As for whistling, who ever whistles anymore, except for those two impertinent notes that signal approval of a dame?

I thought of this recently, wafted from the dental chair on wings of piped-in song. Back home, Doctor Bridge used to whistle as he worked. And though he was no great shakes as a whistler, his whistling had a cheery reassurance I find lacking in canned music, however it's intended to soothe my jangled nerves. Next I entered the supermarket, where I confess I rather enjoyed waltzing my basket down the aisles, loading it with prepackaged groceries to the tune of prepackaged Strauss. Nor could I really resent the dress shop where, lulled no doubt by "Liebestraum," I paid too much for a blouse.

By the time I got to the bank, however, I was beginning to long only to hear the music of some hard, cold cash. But even banks no longer ring and clank with silver dollars, or chuckle with the honest clink of coins. Unless you ask, you get only paper money, dealt out in whispers, as if reluctant to disturb the mood of Mendelssohn.

The payoff came later, however, when I visited our daughter's new high school. There too, in office, library, and study hall, the canned monster was persistently holding forth.

"How can you *concentrate?*" I protested.

"We're so used to it we couldn't concentrate without," she said, "though the stuff we get *is* pretty syrupy." She regarded me with gentle bemusement. "Didn't they even have *music* when you went to school?"

"We certainly did. We sang! Not just in glee club, either. We sang in assembly, and we sang at pep rallies. Everybody sang," I went on, "or made their own music in some way. Or we just kept still and listened. One thing sure, we didn't have music, or what passes for music, poured or dinged and banged constantly into us."

And this was true. Almost every house had an instrument of some kind, and one way to liven up a still evening was to gather 'round and sing. When I was very small, Mother had a parlor organ. The kids would fight over turns to pump up the pedals and pull the stops, or twirl the squealing padded stool to its proper height.

Mother was organist at the church and she practiced every night, while we all joined in. Her hands drew from the softly yielding keys a kind of plaintive, catlike music. The organ breathed and wheezed and had a way of giving off unexpected little moans.

"This darned organ!" Mother would scold it—her way of hinting how much she wanted a piano. All the better homes were getting pianos, elegant dark rectangles on which to drape a fancy scarf and display your vases and photographs. The organ with its little shelves and curlicues and carvings was not only obstinate, but old-fashioned; Grandma and Grandpa had given it to her as a girl. Sometimes she got so mad she'd slap it childishly, or even give it a kick.

We were mad with delight when Mother finally got her piano, as usual for an anniversary. "Sam, Sam, I don't believe it!" She was so excited when the draymen staggered in with the magnificent mahogany thing she almost cried. It had massive Ionic pedestals and dainty little golden feet; it dwarfed and humbled the plain wooden rockers and library table. But it was greeting us with friendly little plinks even before it was set down.

We all made a dash for it and began to bang. Uncle Fred strode in from the kitchen still munching one of his appalling cold gravy sandwiches. He was a gaunt man who read omnivorously, played the Jew's harp, and "chorded," his skeletal hands leaping as he sang forlorn ballads like "The Ship That Never Came Home," or nimble, nonsense ones about polliwogs and mules. His deep-set eyes shone; he could hardly wait.

But, no, Mother must have first turn. In honor of the occasion, she got out her sheet music. Then, deciding that that didn't seem very grateful, she used the hymnal, after all. But what she played was "Joy to the World!" And we sang it as fervently as if it were really Christmas, which it seemed.

Now that we had a piano we too could take lessons, like those princes of privilege we'd watched trudging off with their little satchels. Most kids took from Miss Babcock or Miss Heffner, genteel ladies who smacked your

knuckles with a ruler when necessary. To bear the scars
was a kind of status symbol. But they had long waiting
lists.

Also, there were three of us and not much money.
Mother had already taught us notes on the organ, and
Uncle Fred taught us to sing and chord. So we had a
slight head start when Miss Vally Shorg tripped out to see
us. She "came to the house," she told us, and being new
in town and just getting started would give us a special
rate. We could hardly believe she was a piano teacher;
she looked more like our idea of a chorus girl. Maybe that's
why Dad, in his brash, undaunted way that often embarrassed us, asked for a demonstration. "Oh, happily," she
said—her favorite word. And settling her satin skirts, she
swept one finger the length of the keys—slash! Then all
her fingers with their inch-long nails went clicking and
flying in the gayest, maddest music in the world! Jazz!
"Ain't We Got Fun?" "Yes, We Have No Bananas." "The
Wabash Blues." We sat flabbergasted, enchanted. To learn
to play like that! Of course, she told us, we'd have to start
from the beginning and learn scales, but in time, if we
practiced . . . *Would* we?

Miss Shorg had enormous blue eyes, a laugh like
sleighbells, and she smelled like a fresh bouquet of peonies.
She ratted her blonde hair; she even "painted." And how,
some women wondered, could she *afford* a sealskin coat?
Some parents felt you could trust only prim, dry women
who rapped knuckles and stuck grimly to classical; they
were dubious of anyone who liked kids so much she'd
even come back after supper and play her mad glorious
jazz for their parties. Even show them how to dance! (A
lot of people were still very uneasy about dancing, in-

cluding Mother. Ministers were always thundering against it. But, she reasoned, it couldn't be too harmful in the *home*.)

For one wonderful year we took lessons from Miss Shorg, progressing swiftly from simple exercises to pieces we could really whang away at, like "The Stars and Stripes Forever." But mostly, because we begged so hard, she taught us to "fake." My brother was especially good; he could fake even hymns till they sounded so jazzy you'd want to jump up on the pew and dance. Mother warned him never to try it if he ever was asked to play in church —which wasn't very likely, since he got out of going to church services whenever he could.

When Miss Shorg moved away and got married, there was simply no one to take her place. Thus our musical education ceased. But we continued to love and enjoy the piano even if we couldn't play it as well as we wished. It was a special comfort to Mother, who spent hours at it playing songs like "I'm Lonesome, I Guess That's All" when Dad was out on the road.

Mechanics were already invading music even then. Some people had player pianos. All you had to do was select one of the oblong boxes that looked like stacked firewood, and latch its parchmentlike tube into the opening in front and pump. Magically, ghost hands began moving the keys, and a rain of glittering sound spilled out! By working little levers as well as your feet you could change the tone from bass to treble and add all sorts of orchestral effects. It was like commanding a chorus of angels, or releasing a fairy-tale flock of birds.

Pumping blissfully away at a friend's house, I thought of the four-and-twenty blackbirds baked in the pie. As the cut-out notes moved across the spindled opening you could almost see the little blackbirds flying out, singing madly as they came!

Other very lucky people had phonographs. Our Holmes grandparents, who bought one of the first cars in the county and had also installed the only bathroom for miles around when they lived on the farm, owned an Edison. Their first model had a great horn shaped like a morning glory. On Sundays sometimes after a huge family dinner, the broad double doors to the musty-smelling parlor would be opened and we would be allowed to enter for a concert. Perched in awed suspense upon the horsehair chairs we watched Grandmother select a cylinder, waxy and bright blue, slide it onto the Edison's finger, and with great care set the needle.

Outside we could hear hens clucking, the windmill creaking, horses whinnying in the pasture. While within, from this marvel, came thrilling the voice of Galli-Curci. It was too intensely sweet, it pierced the ears and the very breast like a pain. Or it could be John McCormack, or the incomparable Caruso, whose voice was so powerful it could break a water glass, Grandmother claimed. We could believe it; the giant fern in the bay window seemed to tremble, and the cut-glass pitchers and bowls to rattle in their cabinets.

Later our grandparents moved to town and had the very latest phonograph, a Brunswick, bought after a public demonstration concert at the Presbyterian Church. It had a plumply graceful upright cabinet of burnished wood, hooded with a handsome heavy lid. The music was grooved into thick black platters, to be carefully inserted.

When we visited our grandparents, dutifully and somewhat anxiously before their grandeur, we were never allowed to *touch* the Brunswick, even after we got big.

And its rich product, the voices of Harry Lauder, Madame Schumann-Heink, or a tabernacle choir, always had a quality of formality and bestowal. Whether or not we actually enjoyed them, we listened, we *heard* them, and were impressed.

Lots of people had phonographs—Edisons, Columbias —or Victrolas, which didn't seem so awesome, maybe because they could be called "Vics." Radio was the real marvel now. When our brother came home one night from Tom McCreery's claiming he'd heard an orchestra playing in Omaha, we thought it was one of his crazy jokes. But he got busy reading up on how to build a crystal set. We all hung around eagerly when it was finished and took turns at the earphones listening to the squeals. "I hear something, I hear music!" I lied, partly to please him, partly to confirm my desperate hopes. But it was only our sister Gwen singing in the next room.

It never did work, and years passed before we could afford to buy a radio. Though Grandma and Grandpa got one, with a loudspeaker too, shaped very much like the first arched bell of their Edison.

Meanwhile, to achieve the music we craved, we banged as much as we could out of the piano, or we whistled and sang. Mother sang or whistled as she did her housework. Dad whistled and hummed at his chores. Men and boys whistled, strolling along the streets—but never at girls! When they met a lady, they *stopped* whistling and politely tipped their caps.

And everybody sang—how we sang! We sang at church and we sang at home and we sang every day at school. We sang on hikes and picnics; we sang at parties —in the kitchen making fudge, or gathered around the piano eating it. When there was no one else to play the piano for dancing, or other things were broken down, we sang our own accompaniment.

We sang on dates, in rowboats, canoes, or cars. It was absolutely essential to know the words to all the popular songs, and you were especially lucky if you could harmonize. Luckiest of all if you could also own and play a ukulele.

Clara Bow had helped to popularize this lightweight little instrument. The banjo was also highly favored. From the time we were small, we were always strumming our fingers fervently across lids or pans as we dried the dishes. Or banging with pencils or rulers for drumsticks on make-believe drums. When you are not bombarded with music from other sources every minute, the rhythms that lurk in most of us have the space and the spur to try their wings.

We finally got a radio like everybody else and even a portable phonograph. Many people had predicted that radios would do away with phonographs, but radios crackled with static every time it looked like rain. If you wanted to be sure of music you cranked up the Vic.

Radio even stimulated record sales after a while. You wanted to own some of the lovely pieces you heard orchestras like Guy Lombardo's or Vincent Lopez's playing "direct from Chicago's beautiful Aragon Ballroom." Records could be carted along to add romance to dates. It was not so romantic when, gazing up at the moon and a marvelous guy, Bing Crosby's crooning would descend to guttural grunts. Hastily then your date would have to turn his attention to the rundown Vic and crank 'er up again.

But you didn't really need a Victrola, not if you were in love, or thought so—you could sing! Or just listen to the sounds of romantic night—insects and frogs calling to each other . . . water caressing the sand . . . the tender rustling of the trees, the beat of your own young hearts.

When it came to dance orchestras, the piano and saxophone were fundamental, like the sugar and shortening that starts and enriches a cake, with other musical ingredients added—violin, bass, trumpet, clarinet, drums. And most soloists with dance bands could *sing!* They not only could carry a tune, they had to depend on their own lungs—or like Rudy Vallee, add the collegiate touch of a megaphone. You could hear their actual voices, you could hear the actual music, you could even hear the living, whooshing background of your own dancing feet. And very often as you danced romantically cheek-to-cheek, you and your partner sang too!

Oh, we sang a lot in those days. Silly songs, romantic songs, passionate songs—but songs that were never indiscreet. And we didn't need drink to heighten our joy, embellish our moods (what was so awful about Prohibition, I will always wonder), nor drugs to take us on "trips." We were already on a crazy, glorious, complicated, sometimes desolate, often delicious, always fascinating trip called life. And we didn't want to dim it or miss a moment of it—its songs or its silence. Life invited us to join in its singing. Or when it was silent, to just listen . . . be very still and listen to what it had to say.

XIII

Her Kisses Are Okay,
but How's Her Fudge?

We are so spoiled in this rich country that we've lost the gift of sheer enjoyment—almost nothing is a treat.

Our houses are filled with luxuries; our refrigerators and cupboards overflow. Yet with cakes, cookies, cold cuts, and cheeses to choose from, potato chips and pretzels, snack packs and pickles, seven varieties of TV dinners and nine flavors of ice cream, a son or daughter will complain, "Why don't we ever have anything good to eat?"

One day I marched my adolescent into the supermarket and ordered, "Here, be my guest. You pick it out, get whatever you want." And he wandered around that palace of provender groaning with every conceivable delicacy from every acre of the globe, and finally wheeled back a basket as empty as his face: "*They* don't have anything good either," he mourned.

When in high school, our daughter worked Saturdays at a dress shop so exclusive they practically charge you to look in the windows. Actually the owner was a widow who was having a hard time supporting her family, and there was sometimes little food in her apartment. But one evening our daughter went home with them, and came in later all aglow. "We were so hungry," she said, "and we couldn't find anything to eat but bread and butter and sugar. And tea. Did you ever try bread and butter with sugar on it? It's delicious! Especially with a cup of tea."

I had to laugh. Bread and butter and sugar. Grandpa Griffith used to fix that for us after school. And how good it was, because we were so hungry, as she had been that night. But it took a daughter of this affluent society to remind me how delicious such a simple old-fashioned thing can be.

All children, whatever the era, are born with open mouths. Like yawping birds they demand to be stuffed, especially between meals, and especially with something sweet. When we were kids this oral need was less easily gratified. Mostly we had to be content with an orange or banana from the store in winter, an apple from the cellar, or the fruits that burst in such abundance in the summertime—apples and plums and cherries, blackberries, raspberries, grapes. Mothers baked more then, and we also raided the cookie jar. But treats were something else. Treats were confections, and they played a significant role in the little drama of our lives.

Almost nobody got an allowance (movies had given us the impression that an "allowance" was an arrangement to further spoil rich men's sons) but everybody earned spending money some way, or parents doled it out, sparingly. Even a few pennies were a boon. For there were marvelous penny candies to be chosen, in a blissful torment of indecision, from the display at Triplett's: caramel angels, marshmallow rabbits and tiny cherry-topped marshmallow "ice-cream" cones. An ingenious paraffin bottle filled with sweet red syrup—you not only got to suck the sticky liquid, you could chew the paraffin. A penny also bought you a length of black licorice to snap at people, and to chew gummily, its bitter-sweet juices staining teeth and looking like tobacco juice when you spit.

The first lollipops were called all-day suckers where we lived; those, too, were a penny. Or a jawbreaker, which melted slowly in your swollen cheek until it finally shrank to a sour speck (some people called them sourballs). And for three cents you could buy three woody sticks of licorice root at the Rexall store. It was pale and tough and fibrous and could be masticated for days, its flavor gradually paling like the stringy pulp.

A nickel bought you a genuine ice-cream cone, a candy bar, or a package of gum. The first gum I ever tasted was peppermint, in a pink wrapper, called Yucatan. Shortly thereafter came Juicy Fruit, tasting like the Garden of Eden. Spearmint and Doublemint seemed more for grownups, and Dentyne when it appeared with its spicy bite, the ultimate in sophistication.

We took our gum chewing seriously, often parking a wad on a bedpost overnight, or hiding it under a table. If you were careless about leaving it around, there was no guarantee against raiders; and forlorn indeed was the owner who'd forgotten where he'd put his gum, or lost it to another set of jaws. Indignant before repeated robberies, my sister posted warnings: *"Do Not Take. This is MY GUM! Gwen."*

Nougat Bars were our introduction to candy bars. A trade name, I believe, for those divine rectangles of chocolate filled with creamy maple and walnuts. But to Dad all bars thereafter, O'Henrys, Hersheys, Baby Ruths, continued to be "noogat bars," to be brought home and presented to Mother. "Here, kiddo, brought you a little treat."

It was a scene endlessly repeated: "A treat, a treat, Dad's brought us a treat!" Instantly, joy and celebration became as tangible as the contents of those mysteriously rattling sacks.

Dad had a stern and happy code of his own devising: Since he smoked cigars, and whiled away many a happy hour at Mack's Cigar Store and Pool Hall, he thought his family deserved a compensating indulgence; he brought us treats. Mother never scolded about the pool hall; he didn't drink and he never stayed late, and no matter how tough the times she was convinced that men needed these diversions. "Dad works so hard for all of us," she would say. She did sometimes get uneasy about the candy, however. "Sam, you really shouldn't, it's all I can do right now to scare up money for the collection at Ladies Aid." So he took to announcing, with a twinkle, "Look what I won playing Snooker," as he tossed her the sack. It became a family joke that our dad was the best Snooker player in town.

When times were prosperous and he had been on the road, he often brought her a whole box of chocolates in a fancy box. We swarmed around, awed before the sheer elegance of the box, wanting to hold it, shake it, sniffing at its dark treasures even before they were revealed in their crinkly nests. Dizzy before the choices, and desperately planning strategy to possess the box. How lavish, how sumptuous the beauty of those candy boxes with their painted scenes, their paper lace and roses and ribbons—always an enormous satin-bow ribbon. How marvelous they were for storing handkerchiefs, trinkets, paper dolls; and a collection of fancy candy boxes was a status symbol for girls, whatever their age.

You could generally count on treats on Friday nights

when the *Saturday Evening Post* arrived. Dad would stroll downtown after supper for a friendly game before the magazines were pitched off the 8:13. He was usually first in line when they were hauled over to the newsstand from the depot on a handtruck, generally pulled by Leo Baker, our hardworking "town idiot," whom everybody loved. When Dad got home he smelled not only of cigars and the fat shiny new magazine under his arm, but the big striped sack in his pocket. For his final stop would be the Greek's Candy Kitchen.

This was our night for reading aloud. Especially in winter when the hard-coal burner clucked and hissed and shed its rosy glow. Sometimes the sack would be stuffed with marshmallows, fluffy white cushions dusty with powdered sugar or brown with toasted coconut. Rejoicing, we would run for the long forks while Mother drew up the rockers and leafed through the pages. And while she and Dad picked the first story, we would open the isinglass door and roast the marshmallows over the coals.

More often the treat was an assortment of rich mouthmelting bonbons made fresh that day. Sprawled on the floor, we would give ourselves over to their bliss, while Mother's voice wove enchantment through the words of Jack London, Edna Ferber, William Hazlett Upson, Gene Stratton Porter, Booth Tarkington, Zane Grey. We suffered in the Klondike, won the Golden West, laughed until we rolled on the floor over the Earthworm tractors of Alexander Botts; we scared ourselves with mysteries and murders, our hearts broke with the exquisite pangs of love.

Outside, the wind might be howling; a few feet away our bedrooms would be stone-cold. But here in the snug circle of the family, here in the firelight, we were warm, safe, feasting on delight.

In summer, treats could also be bought if you had the money, from Mr. Wilson, a forerunner of today's Good Humor man. Mr. Wilson traversed the streets at twilight with his horse-drawn vehicle, half-buggy, half-wagon. He too clanged a bell, whose tantalizing call was heightened by the rhythmic clop of Dolly's hooves. Hearing it dimly in the distance kids for blocks halted their games of Run, Sheep, Run and streaked for home, there sweatily to assault their parents rocking on porches.

"Please, *please!*" Hearts pounded as the magical sounds drew nearer and parents still hesitated. It was almost dark, he was almost upon you, soon it would be too late. "I'll hoe the garden tomorrow, I'll beat the rugs . . . please!"

What pain when Dad would shake his head, say firmly if always a bit forlornly, "No, I'm sorry, we just can't." But when, sighing, he would reach into his pocket, what relief. And what a joy to dart back to the curb and stand, often surrounded by envious friends, flagging Dolly to a halt. Sometimes Dad trudged along and visited with Mr. Wilson while you climbed the iron step and poked your head into his fragrant caravan smelling of Juicy Fruit and Hershey bars and buttery dairy odors. Fireflies flashed their fairy lanterns, night things chirped, the whole world seemed to sing and glow as you returned across the dew-wet grass, ecstatically licking an ice-cream cone. Or carrying a whole carton of the precious stuff.

Ice cream . . . How can any child of today's crammed freezers imagine the thrill those words evoked? The cartons were square with a fold-down top and a little wire handle. Your father would surprise everybody by appearing with a quart for the family on a hot afternoon. "Ice cream, ice cream!" the word spread, while Mother got out the cut-glass dishes, the spoons. "Now come quick, get started before it melts." Not that we needed urging, we were pressing in upon her, jealously watching the size of portions, grabbing the biggest if we could.

Some people had ice-cream freezers and made their own. Mostly people on farms who could be profligate with cream. Churches made ice cream, too, for picnics and ice-cream socials on the lawn. Making ice cream was a lot of trouble but worth it in sheer anticipation. You had to have dry ice, which smoked and would burn you if you touched it, and plenty of coarse grainy salt. The mixture of cream and sugar and vanilla was put in a metal container which was packed in this and vigorously cranked. An arduous process that could go on for hours, it seemed.

Everybody took turns cranking, which became harder and harder as the mixture thickened. If you quit too soon it would be soupy and irretrievable. At last when arms could bear no more the frosty, bitter-cold lid was pried open, the paddles worked out. Lip-smacking kids pranced about, clamoring to lick the paddles, and the winner hastened off, sometimes using a finger as well as his triumphant tongue.

Some people went a little out of their senses at the sight of a whole freezer full of ice cream. They stood waiting, not with sauce dishes in hand, but huge serving bowls. One of our cousins consumed six of these at a sitting, I remember, and later when everyone else was surfeited went back and cleaned up the can, at least another quart. Even church picnics were veritable ice-cream orgies for the young.

Homemade ice cream was generally a man's province; woman's was homemade candy, and rare was the house where at least once a week somebody didn't make fudge.

Fudge was delicious and actually most people's favorite, but other kinds lent more prestige. The lady who produced a platter of fondant, panoche, or cream-white (sometimes even pastel-tinted) divinity to the candy table at the church bazaar was fussed over and enjoyed a distinction never achieved by the contributor of even the creamiest, nut-studded fudge.

Mother never went in for exotic high jinks in the kitchen; she settled for the staple fudge: two cups of sugar, two heaping tablespoons of cocoa, a cup of milk, a dab of butter, stir, cook, and call the children when "the little dogs are bubbling up." Tumbling over each other like puppies ourselves we would rush to the stove, jumping or being lifted to gaze upon the seething mahogany mass.

"It's done when it spins a thread." We always saw the thread half a dozen times before she shared the vision. Then she would remove from the fire, beat swiftly and pour into a buttered pie tin, and the battle royal would ensue over who got to lick the spoon and pan.

Every little girl learned to make fudge almost as soon as she could stand on a chair and stir a batch. It was a part of her social training. It helped immeasurably when friends came to spend the evening, especially boys.

The undisputed fudge queen of our neighborhood was Gert Beatty, who added certain aristocratic touches in keeping with her family status. She spurned anything except real cream, lots of real butter, squares of bitter chocolate, and a dollop of Karo syrup. Sometimes, at our impassioned insistence, she crossed the street where we had managed to assemble these ingredients in our humble kitchen, and there demonstrated her art. She cooked her fudge very carefully over low heat, stirring every minute, and would have none of the thread-spinning method. Hers was to drop bits into a cup of cold water and see if it formed a little ball. This seemed to us a very classy touch. Furthermore, she added the butter last and let the fudge cool *before* beating. When it was deemed cool enough she took up the spoon and there began an endurance contest of beating that went on until arms dropped. Her timing was perfect; at the precise moment when it would have hardened to ruin in the pan, Gert dumped. Pressed flat with buttered fingers and swiftly marked, that fudge was so impossibly rich and luscious it would have pleasured the gods.

Gert also taught us how to make taffy, which was messy and difficult but fun. Buttering your hands, you took a fistful of the cooked, sticky, gooey concoction and pulled. It got all over the kitchen and us; the candy that resulted was brittle and jaw-breaking; but taffy pulling was a great way to liven up an evening, and so was popping corn. Sometimes, pouring the still sticky taffy syrup over the white explosions in the dishpan, we made popcorn balls.

By the time we were going into our teens, we swarmed in and out of each other's houses, and there was always the fragrance of something cooking or popping. Concocting these treats was a mode of entertainment, along with playing the piano, singing, dancing (or trying to learn), stunts, and playing cards. And at some time during the evening, usually early to get things going, people would head for the kitchen. Boys didn't have much money to spend and there weren't many places to spend it if they had (the movies, the roller skating rink, and Saturday night dances when we were old enough, just about covered the possibilities). So girls entertained at home. Parents were usually present; they might have strolled or driven down to the movies, or gone to choir practice, but they were never gone long and were never too far off the scene.

Boys donned aprons or tied dishtowels around their waists and helped make the candy, or shook the corn popper. There was much yelling and spilling and laughing and chasing, and many trips to the back porch to beat the fudge, or see if it was firm enough to eat. In winter the back porch, even tar paper-enclosed, was very cold, but the fervent beating of your arms, and often your heart as other arms went around you, kept you warm. In summer you lingered, perched on the railing beneath the vines, picking out the constellations, counting falling stars, and necking with a breathless innocence and joy.

We savored caresses, I am convinced, in a way that must be inconceivable to today's sex-saturated youth. Because we had to work for things and wait for things we cherished things. Our kisses, like our confections, were exciting and always a little marvelous.

They too were a treat!

XIV

A Lizzie, My Love and You

Wasn't it President Herbert Hoover who once promised this country a chicken in every pot and two cars in every garage? Poor dear Mr. Hoover! Despite the depression that temporarily plucked those chickens and detoured those cars, he lived to see what he predicted—and more. Today it's not only "chicken every Sunday," it's chicken practically every day. As for the average middle-class American—if the family only owns *two* cars it's considered almost underprivileged. There's Dad's car, Mother's car, the station wagon for the country, and the cars for everybody else old enough to have a driver's license. Not to mention the ailing jalopies its teen-age mechanics are forever hauling home to practice on.

If there's an antique car buff in the family, you're also likely to find a Stutz or a Duesenberg enthroned, or a Model T being lovingly polished and tuned. While, in addition to all the four-wheeled vehicles, a motorcycle or two often claims its parking place. At our house, in fact, there's always such a traffic jam in the backyard it's hard sometimes to get out of the driveway. And maneuver out of it a mother must—to transport both herself and any underage progeny to the endless meetings, lessons, and social events which plague suburban society and make her, as one friend puts it, "the modern female centaur—half woman, half station wagon." . . .

When I was a very little girl, the woman who actually drove an automobile was a rare and dashing creature. In fact an auto or "machine" was at one time a novel and impressive thing. My grandfather Holmes was fond of recalling the day Uncle Frank telephoned to announce that he was driving out to the farm in a "machine." Neighbors listening in on the party line were so excited they phoned the news to anybody else who might have missed it, and lined up beside the country road to await his arrival.

He was a long time coming, having caused a runaway on the road, and had several breakdowns. But at last the clouds of dust and the awful noise proclaimed his approach. He swung into the barnyard like Phaethon and his fiery steeds, scattering squawking hens, causing horses to rear, and the hired man nearly to fall off the windmill.

Cars soon became a common sight around town, although owned mostly by the privileged, such people as doctors, judges, and bankers; farmers were beginning to buy Flivvers, or Tin Lizzies, as the first Fords were called. You almost never saw a horse and buggy, although horse-drawn wagons were hitched up on side streets where the mealy-smelling feed stores stood. And "The Iceman Cometh" still meant the jingle of harness and the slow clop of hooves, while the milkman, the junk man, and a few of the delivery wagons from the grocery stores depended upon the horse to draw their simple cargo up the sunny alleys and along the shady streets. And the squeak of leather, the creak of wooden wheels, the rich vinegar tang of horseflesh and the sound of thick teeth wrenching grass were a part of childhood itself, warmly sweet and enthralling.

"But how did you *get* places?" my offspring demand.

"We walked," I tell them. "Ever hear of it? We used our feet."

For a vast network of sidewalks encompassed every small town. And everybody used them. To children, particularly, those sidewalks were a constant source of interest and concern. "Step on a crack you break your mother's back." You raced each other madly to the corners where the "good lucks" were (the imprint of a builder's name) and stamped on them. Sidewalks held seed pods to be squirted in the spring, and were rich with gold and scarlet leaves in the fall. In summer some were so hot to your bare feet you had to walk on the cool, tickling grass. In winter you slid joyously on the icy ones—against parental warnings about wearing out your shoes. Brothers were always having to shovel snowy sidewalks, girls being sent forth with brooms to sweep them. The condition of the sidewalk going past your house was of vast concern to mothers. Mine always contended that "a slovenly sidewalk is the first sign of a slovenly house." And of course all the kids knew the choicest sidewalks for roller skating— the long, smooth stretches where you practically flew, wheels purring; the ones with the jagged, broken places where you must daringly jump; the ones so bumpy you took to the grass, clump-clump-clump.

Adults also depended on the sidewalks. Men walked to work in the morning and walked home for big boiled dinners at noon. And after the dishes were done and the dishtowels were drying on the back porch, their wives got dressed up and walked to Tuesday Club or Missionary Society or Ladies Aid. Whole families walked downtown to the movies after supper, or to the band concert in Sunset Park on Sunday afternoon. Boys walked girls home from church or library, and young couples strolled romantically along the lakeshore in the moonlight, arms entwined. We lived quite near the lake; and like the child in Stevenson's poem I often lay reluctant to go to sleep, hearing that poignant preview to life itself—"The grownup people's feet—still going by me on the street."

But more and more it became the cars going by. Oh, those lucky ones, those divinely favored—the people who owned cars! My grandparents had moved to town by now and possessed a handsome Hudson touring car, although neither of them drove it. The chauffering was done by Aunt Ada, who had learned some years before by simply going down to the garage where Uncle Frank stored his "machine" and informing the men there that he had sent her for it. She was a school teacher, dazzlingly beautiful. Although no woman in the entire county had ever been known to drive, the combination overpowered them. Whatever their misgivings, they cranked it up, flung open the doors, and watched her go jouncing off. When Uncle Frank sauntered in shortly thereafter and learned what had happened, they all paled. "You fools, if she kills herself I'll sue you!" Instead, she returned elated. One of them was so relieved he rushed off to be sick.

Aunt Ada took Grandmother out riding almost every day, and on rare and signal occasions they would invite us. To go for a ride with anybody was a big treat, but with Grandma it was positively awesome. She dressed in crackling taffeta and lacy shawls, and the diamonds in her ears sparkled like Aunt Ada's wit. We were almost too dazzled to enjoy it.

It was fitting that Grandma and Grandpa have a Golden Wedding. Not many people lived that long, and the whole town helped celebrate. Their twelve children arrived from far-flung places and bought them a solid-gold pitcher and tray with twelve golden goblets. There was a feast worthy of Belshazzar. Most impressive of all was the fact that Aunt Barbara's family, who had vast holdings on the west coast, had driven clear across country by car! And what a car—the first sedan most of us had ever seen. With its tasseled window shades and cut-glass bud vases —a veritable limousine. To ride in it was to positively wallow in reflected glory.

Oh, to own a car. Just any kind of car, like practically everybody else was getting. It wouldn't have to be a Dodge or an Overland or a Hupmobile; a Ford would be just dandy. How we envied the tourists who poured through town, camping by the lakeshore. You could spot them by their glamorous outfits. Khaki, because of the dusty roads. Brimmed khaki hats and shirts and skirts, khaki knickers. Some of the bolder women wore knickers and allowed their daughters to, claiming, defensively, that they were more practical for traveling . . . Traveling! To cross state lines, head for distant and exotic places like the Badlands of South Dakota or even Yellowstone Park. Sometimes the cars flaunted self-kidding signs: CALIFORNIA OR BUST! The daring, the wonder—for they must climb mountains, brave deserts—and breakdowns and flat tires were accepted hazards among these knowing pioneers.

Storm Lake people too set off on these fabulous journeys, with luggage strapped to the fenders, tents roped on top, and the cheers and jokes of envious stay-at-homes in their ears. And to witness such a departure and only turn back to the humming blue haze of your own dumb yard was to suffer a consuming ache, a wild inchoate longing that could only be appeased by wheels.

And then Dad bought a car. I lay awake straining to hear him discussing the possibility with Mother one night, and praying. And the thrill when he actually came driving up in it for her to look over cannot be conveyed. It was, to be sure, a Lizzie, and secondhand. But its black tin sides were shiny, its canvas top a trifle imperious, propped high on its skinny arms. He sprang out jauntily, cap on the back of his head, face aglow. "Well, Mama, what d'you think?"

She was startled and timorous. "Oh, Sam, I've been wondering, can we really afford it?" (They were still paying on the note at the bank for his share of the solid-gold goblets.) "And—can you *drive* it?"

"Drive it? Can I *drive* it?" He threw back his head and laughed. Can birds fly? Can fish swim? Like most of his big rollicking family, he had been born knowing how to do grand, magnificent things. He strolled around it, fondly kicked a tire. The way he figured it, he told her, a traveling salesman almost had to have a car. This way he'd actually save money, not have to stay in hotels so often. He could get home lots more nights to be with the family. He hugged her and sniffed, in a little way he had, at her heavy black hair. They were very much in love, a fact of which we were blissfully unconscious, though it enriched our lives. What he was really telling her was that he could be home with her more often.

"Get in, come on now, I'll take you for a spin."

"Oh, my goodness, I look a sight! Wait—" She hurried into the house to put on hat, coat and gloves, though it was a warm day. Meanwhile, half the neighborhood came running, thunderstruck. Kids swarmed all over the hot, leathery smelling upholstery, begging to go too, and of course to sit in the front seat. But no, that was reserved for Mother. Dad elegantly handed her in. She sat stiff and pale while he cranked up. Yank. Yank. Yank. A ferocious and seemingly futile undertaking.

Still emanating optimism, he trudged back, leaned inside to adjust the spark lever, pull the choke. More earnest jerks of the handle that protruded in front like an impudent tongue. He was beginning to perspire, and so was Mother in her Sunday best. She implored him not to strain himself. She could see on his pinkening face the gritting of teeth and tightening of lips that presaged an oath. Instead, he paused, mopping his brow, and lifting one side of the radiator, made mysterious adjustments within. Then, pressing bodily against his adversary, he gave the crank his all. Victory came with a few gasps, a mighty throat clearing, a roar so thunderous Dad had to leap aside. We all held on while he rushed around, vaulted in, yanking at levers, stepping on pedals, releasing brakes. We were off, down the shady streets of morning, with neighbors looking up from gardens and clotheslines to remark our triumphant departure. And Dad, to Mother's distress, further shattered the peace by loudly honking the rubber horn.

Whenever Dad was home there was no greater pleasure than to clamber into that dusty chariot and go for a ride. Mother often adjured us not to tease. "Dad's tired, he's been driving all week, remember." But he was always a good sport about it. We drove along the familiar streets and parks that flanked the lake. We drove past

the canning factory. Sometimes we drove to Alta, a neighboring town, and stopped for ice-cream cones. Sometimes,
if we teased hard, we drove clear to Aurelia or Cherokee,
beyond it. The gravel road pinged and crunched beneath the tires; the wind tore gloriously through as we sped
along at the insane speed of thirty-five miles an hour.

"Now, Sam, be careful," Mother would worry, "don't
meet anybody on that bridge just up ahead." Bridges were
narrow and treacherous, over all the little gullies and
creeks. For two cars to try and cross them at the same
time could be disastrous.

We rode on hot green summer afternoons, when the
sun was paving the lake with diamonds or laying its
lonely loveliness over the pastures and fields. We went
riding in the cool of the evening, with sunset still lingering in the sky, and rode, just rode till the stars came out.
This miracle of movement, to be carried by some force
other than your own, how divine. And the fact that we
were all together, Mother, Dad, the kids, and usually some
nice old soul who otherwise never got out, added to its
cozy consequence.

Almost immediately, even as today, our next passionate objective was to learn to drive. This happened with
almost alarming ease. Drivers' licenses had not yet been
invented. Anyone tall enough to reach the pedals and the
steering wheel at the same time could. You learned by
watching your father; or grimly, guttily, he taught you—
and the battle royal was on as to who *got* the car even
before it had cooled off at the curb and your weary parent
trudged up the walk. Once this happened, you didn't want
to ride with your folks, you wanted to "joyride," which
meant gathering a load of your peers and heading for a
dance, a skating rink, or wickedly, a Sunday night movie,

forbidden in Storm Lake, but available in some distant village of iniquity. Or—you just rode. And parked.

Ministers inveighed against joyriding as they did against dancing and cards. And a true inspiration of the devil it sometimes seemed to be. Especially in winter. Cars, once put up on blocks at the first snowfall, were now able to negotiate most main roads. Providing you first thawed them out with kettles of boiling water and didn't break an arm getting them to start. (Self-starters couldn't be depended on; every car still jutted its ornery but essential crank.) Then there was the trial of keeping icy side curtains buttoned down. Fiendish winds tore through the cracks in the isinglass. The wintry sins of joyriding were overrated—heaterless, bundled three feet deep in boots, blankets, mittens, ear muffs, and scarves —they were simply too hard to achieve!

Also, winter or summer, tires were always blowing out and your date had to jack up the car, wrench off the tire, examine the limp, ailing inner tube, scrape it, and then whack out a bright rubber patch to glue over its punctured flesh. Then he got out the pump and vigorously gave it artificial respiration. When it no longer wheezed, it was squeezed prayerfully back into the tire and the tire put back on the rim. Meanwhile, you froze by slow graceful inches in the car; or you got a quick deep freeze— and the reputation of being a good sport—by crawling painfully out and helping.

Blowouts were even more frequent in summer. The fierce Iowa heat and the blazing gravel were more than the strained, oft-patched lungs could endure—bang! they'd simply explode. Throughout the rescue operations you sweltered, sweat, and gasped sweet nothings at each other through clouds of dust kicked up by luckier vehicles.

Between the patches on the side-curtains and the patches on the inner tubes, courting by car was a mad, gay, colorful, courageous undertaking. (My dad, incidentally, invented a wonderful glue for both patching purposes and augmented the family income with it until closed cars and spare wheels with tires intact made these earlier remedies obsolete.)

Coupes and sedans were replacing touring cars. Henry Ford had astounded and shocked the world by abandoning Lizzie. Yes, Lizzie—cheap, faithful, fruitful Lizzie, who had borne him so many customers so long. He was replacing her with some young hussy to be called a Model A—and it seemed a kind of betrayal. Great secrecy prevailed. No pictures were released. And at the local Ford agency all windows were draped until the proper day. Whether in mourning or for wedding veils was hard to say. Then you met the bride—and grinned, in a kind of reluctant relief. She was beautiful, most people agreed, "but still a Ford." Which meant something sturdy and economical and comfortably middle class. In short, American.

Many women were driving by then, and practically all their offspring, but few families boasted more than one car. There were no parking problems around our high school. Only the consolidated schools had school buses. We cosmopolitan town kids walked—even home for lunch, no matter how far we lived. After school we either walked in big, noisy bunches, or we bummed rides with the country kids who had to drive to get there. Or we swarmed over those other rare favorites of the gods who actually owned or had daily access to a car. Any parent rich or doting enough to provide it could convey instant popularity; overnight the plainest child could become a veritable Valentino or the school queen.

This will always be true to some degree. But it was infinitely more so then than today when a car is regarded not only as a status symbol, but practically a civil right!

With college, of course, the mysteries of distance vanished, the boundaries melted. We married and joined a mobile society, where parents spend half their waking hours on wheels; where children learn to dance and swim and ski, but don't learn to walk. "Going for a ride" cannot possibly hold the thrill for our youngsters that it had for us. Yet there is still something warm and wonderful about the family's piling into the car and setting off—for the supermarket, a drive in movie, or a long vacation trip (do spite the murder and mayhem that often occur on the back seat). Dad or Mother or a tall son driving. Young friends along, or some nice neighbor who otherwise might not get out for a ride.

The cars are big glass and steel splendors now, the highways broad and smooth, the hazards less from breakdowns and flat tires than traffic and speed. Yet something old-fashioned and eternal and curiously American remains. The sheer pleasure of locomotion—to view the world through moving windows . . . that new housing development, that bend in the road, that mountain, that lake . . . and do it with those you love.

XV

"Supper's Ready!"

Whatever happened to the family dinner hour? Or "supper" as we called it in our small town? That time at the end of the day when everybody was summoned to wash up and sit down together to share a common meal. A time not only to eat but to talk to each other, even if you sometimes quarreled. A time and place where you could laugh, joke, exchange ideas, tell stories, dump your troubles. (Yes, and learn your manners.)

Surely its disappearance has a lot to do with the much lamented disintegration of the American family. We've traded it in on the TV set and a freezer stuffed with prepack foods. We've exchanged it gaily for the cocktail hour. We've let it get lost in the flurry of meetings, lessons, parties, and activities to which we have mortgaged our evenings today. None of these things are particularly harmful in themselves, most in fact are essentially progressive and pleasant. But nonetheless an insidious encroachment and ultimately the destroyer of a daily custom that could not but contribute to family solidarity.

"Suppertime!" The last meal of the day . . .

Only city folks or people who put on city airs called it dinner. To us dinner was at noon, and we didn't mean lunch, we meant *dinner*. When we spoke of three square meals a day we meant three square meals. During the morning, along with everything else she had to do, a woman was also getting dinner. Tending the pot roast or pounding the beefsteak, cooking the vegetables and potatoes, making a custard and opening a Mason jar of pears or home-canned applesauce. And promptly on the stroke of twelve it had to be ready. For at that point the town's activities would come to a sudden halt with the blasting of the noon whistle at the firehouse.

On that instant stores and offices closed, school got out. A few doctors and lawyers and businessmen ate at Martin's Cafe or the Bradford Hotel, but most men headed for home. Since we had no school cafeterias or buses we walked home too—only the country kids, whom we envied, were allowed to bring their lunches. Winter or spring, fair weather or foul, we walked; and since our house was more than a mile away, it was stow away all that food and start back so you wouldn't be late. (To be tardy was a disgrace.) Anyway, noon dinner in our town was an hour of suspended activity, except for a sense of clicking dishes and earnestly munching jaws.

Supper was different. More leisurely. Less a time of common refueling than an hour when everybody gathered at the day's end to summarize and share what had gone on. And it varied with families. You'd begin to hear the calls, "Hey, kids, come on now, time to help get supper—" or the announcement, "Supper's ready!" all over the neighborhood anywhere from five o'clock on. People like the Renshaws ate early; Mr. Renshaw worked the night shift at the creamery and liked a long evening with his family before he donned his white overalls and departed. Judge J. Rutherford Jensen was to be seen stalking up the steps between the white Corinthian columns of his house at 5:15, expecting his food to be on the table and his children ready to sit down. Mrs. Flanders who liked to gad and was sort of slapdash about her cooking never managed to round up her brood until nearly seven o'clock—to the horror of some women and the distress of many kids, because most of us had finished the dishes by then and were ready to play out again.

But whether you ate at five or six or seven, one thing we had in common: Everybody had to *be* there. And in most households everybody had to help.

We thought the boys got off easy after we'd converted to cooking with gas. Before that they'd had to chop the kindling for the range, carry in the baskets of mealy red cobs, and from dusky bins in the basement haul up the snout-mouthed coal buckets. Theirs too the duty of trimming the wicks on the oilstove, cleaning its yellowed isinglass chimneys, and filling its tank with kerosene poured from a can with a potato stuck on its spout. Since Mother didn't quite trust her gas stove, especially for baking, they still sometimes had to. And after supper they had to carry out the scraps.

Even very little girls were summoned in to put the teakettle on and start the potatoes. Potatoes were as essential to supper as the silverware. Boiled potatoes or fried; for company scalloped or mashed; but inevitably potatoes. And since you'd usually had them boiled for dinner and there were generally plenty left over, the cold, boiled globes were chopped up, salted, peppered, and fried.

Mother was not an impassioned cook. She felt a de-

fensive, half-guilty distress for women who spent most of
their time in the kitchen. "All that work just for something
to put in your mouth and swallow, just to fill your stomach,
just to *eat*." To her, food for the soul was just as important, and she feasted richly, if indiscriminately, on Tenny-
son and Tarkington, Shakespeare and Grace Noll Crowell
and Harold Bell Wright. A true "book drunk," as she described herself, she would often become so absorbed that
it would be late afternoon before she came to, shocked
to discover from the redolent odors wafting up and down
the block that other people's suppers were cooking. "Oh,
dear, what'll we have?" she would worry vaguely, and
start summoning offspring for calculations and tasks.

If in summer, someone would be dispatched to pick,
pull, or dig whatever was ready from the garden, and
fingers would fly, snapping, shelling, or peeling things.
Meanwhile, tapping her gold tooth, she would achieve a
small list of items for when the phone would ring and
whoever was downtown would ask, "What do you want
for supper?" Often she dismissed the whole business with
a cheerful, "Oh, I don't care, just whatever looks good."

Dad didn't mind and he bought with a lavish hand
when he could. If times were plentiful the meat was in-
variably thick red beefsteak, and the sack would be full of
surprises like Nabiscos and coconut-topped marshmallow
cookies, along with cherry pie from the bakery, and white
grapes. And maybe a fresh hairy coconut, which we broke
open with a hammer, drinking its flat tasteless milk and
prying out its sweet if tough white heart.

We were always ravenous by suppertime, and no
matter what was served we fell on it with relish. Especially
on the days when the bread was fresh from the oven.
Though Mother would never win any ribbons at the

county fair and didn't want to, she did make good bread. And like everybody else (except the elite who could afford the extravagance of bakery bread) she was forced to bake it once a week.

The batter had to be mixed and set to rise the night before. A great, yeasty, bubbling batch in a huge granite pan. Potato water was saved to combine with the scalded milk, salt, sugar, and lard, and into this she sifted white cones of flour. We often knelt on kitchen chairs to watch, begging to help by shaking the heavy, squeaking flour sifter. When the dough was thick and smooth it was covered with a lid and left to rise on the lingering warmth at the back of the stove. If the house was cold, Mother would tuck it down as cozily as she could under a heavy towel.

By morning it would have blossomed tall and white, only to be stirred down and forced to accept more flour. Now she must dump it onto a floured board and knead it, flopping the tough yet delicate mass over and over, pressing out the air bubbles that made little squealing protests, caressing it, yet maneuvering it to her will. And thus subdued it was set to rise again.

By afternoon it was ready to be kneaded once more and molded into loaves. When we were small she always pinched off enough dough to let us play with and to fashion into tiny loaves of our own. They were usually grubby from our hands, but they looked beautiful waiting on the sunny windowsill in the little lids that served as pans. When the loaves themselves had risen, she brushed their plump heads with melted butter and popped them into an oven so hot that sometimes the lids on the range were as rosy as rouged cheeks.

Slowly the heavenly smell of baking bread began to

drift through the house. When you came in from school or play your jaws leaked and you began to tease, "When will the bread be done?"

"Well, it should be soon." Opening the nickel-plated door, she would reach in and snap an experimental finger on the brown cracking crust. "Just a few more minutes." Finally, clutching a dish towel, she would reach in and carefully draw out the large black pan. The loaves were dumped on the table, to stand tall and golden as the sheaves of wheat from which the flour had come. Promptly she brushed them with more butter, and they took on a satin sheen. When she broke them apart, their white flesh steamed.

"Now don't eat too much," she would warn as people begged for more. "Hot bread isn't good for the stomach. Besides, I don't want you to spoil your supper."

On rare occasions she diverted part of the batch into cinnamon rolls, a special treat. But the fresh bread itself eaten straight from the oven with butter, or slavered with honey or strawberry jam or apple butter, was enough to rouse the envy of the gods.

In a day or two it was simply bread, no longer so white and a trifle heavy, to be cut on a breadboard with a sawtoothed knife before each meal. And you disloyally wished you could buy bakery bread like some people, it seemed so light and spongy beside your mother's sturdy product.

Mother also made a marvelous bread pudding dignified by the name of "chocolate soufflé." Dry bread soaked in scalded milk; sugar, cocoa, vanilla and a couple of eggs added. Baked in a moderate oven until a knife came clean and its rich chocolaty promise was scarcely to be borne. The crowning touch was the hard sauce, which one of us always made. Confectioners' sugar was stirred into about half a cup of butter, added and pressed and added and pressed until you achieved a fat white ball that could literally take no more. (Also a few drops of vanilla.) Then you made it into individual balls, and stamped on each, with the bottom of a cut-glass toothpick holder, the imprint of a diamond or a daisy or a star. Bread pudding? Nonsense. These creamy balls, melting down over each crusty steaming dish, achieved ambrosia.

But whatever we ate for supper, whether the fare was feast or famine, certain rules prevailed: The whole family ate in the dining room, on a linen cloth with linen napkins. Nobody ever sat down before Mother. And nobody ever left the table unless she excused him first. Nor did we ever begin until everyone was present and until the blessing was asked. Also, we all had to sit straight in our chairs, left hand in the lap. No reaching, no stooping or slurping, and every request prefaced by "please." Mother believed in the old saw: "Always eat as if you were dining with the king, then you'll never be embarrassed if the king comes to dine."

After manners, we shed all pretense of trying to please the king. We were noisy—oral, vocal, clamorous, everybody trying to tell what had happened to *him* today. "Don't talk with your mouth full," Mother kept admonishing. "Don't all try to talk at once." It was futile; good or bad we were dying to spill it at the family table, where we knew reactions would be fervent. The best times were when everybody was in a good mood and the tales were funny. We laughed, sometimes so hard we had to be excused. Dad and my brothers were all incurable clowns; given the slightest encouragement they did what they could to bring this about. Sometimes we burst into song.

"Now we don't sing at the table" was another somewhat futile admonition. When people who enjoy each other's company get together it's hard to curb such a spontaneous expression.

Not that harmony always prevailed. The king would have been shocked at the vehemence of our arguments, the sound and fury of our quarrels. When the yelling got too bad Mother would simply say firmly, "I think you'd better be excused." The only things we were not free to discuss at the table were matters which might turn the stomach. No gory details of accidents or operations, no mention of creatures that crawled. If anyone slipped, Dad would pale slightly, clap a napkin to his mouth and flee without even asking Mother.

Other than this, the family's evening meal was a kind of funfest, open forum, wailing wall, and free-for-all. A place where you laughed or complained about your unfair teacher or got very mad and had things out with somebody without missing a bite, or, as far as I know, getting indigestion. A place so lively and filled with possibilities, in fact, that nobody wanted to miss it . . .

Today's experts warn that only agreeable subjects should be discussed at the family dinner table. I suppose I must agree. If and when you can *find* a table with an entire family gathered around it of an evening, the occasion is so rare it ought not to be marred with dissension. I have also read articles describing a kind of protocol of participation. Mother or Father suggests, "Now let's all go around the table and each of us tell the most interesting thing that happened to him or that he's learned today." This too I have tried, with discouraging results. "Aw, nothing much," one child will shrug. Or another, "Sorry, I've got to get going, Mike's picking me up—" While another is intent only poking down the absolute minimum required before escaping back to his programs.

No, the call "Supper's ready!" doesn't echo through neighborhoods much any more. It's dinner now in most places, and it's seldom ready for everybody at the same time. In the first place, Mother's not always there to get it. She's not home from work yet, or the golf course or her club; but there's plenty of food in the refrigerator, or the kids can heat up a nourishing four-course TV dinner, they won't starve. Or Dad's late getting home, and what with bucking traffic after a hard day he needs to unwind a bit. So the clever wife already has the martinis ready, and they share their Happy Hour while the kids eat in the kitchen or the rec room in front of the TV set.

In fact a lot of young wives recommend this as one way to keep a good marriage going. "I always feed the children first; then Jim and I can enjoy a quiet dinner without all that confusion. We need to be able to talk to each other, we need adult conversation."

Well, fine, good—don't we all? But aren't we already reaping a sorry but logical harvest of kids who were herded off the scene to communicate only with each other, and so can have no meaningful dialogue with adults now? Or who sat transfixed (as children are squatting still) before cartoons and Westerns and wars. No wonder so many of them are violent and destructive, so many of them rude. And how about their manners? How can you learn to sit or stand up straight while slouched on the floor? Who teaches you not to slurp or behave crudely or refrain from discussing the dissection of a worm while eating, if at the same time you're downing a solitary dinner to the accompaniment of pools of blood in living color?

Suppertime . . . That final meal when the day was almost over. The tradition of the family table. In letting it slip away from us I'm afraid we've lost something precious. We've cheated our children, stunted their social growth, gagged their articulation, cut off too early those ties that nature meant for us. The ties that bind us to people in the same family, people who represent comfort, security, nourishment, not only of body but of spirit. Ties that used to be gathered up at the close of day and drawn together, if not always in peace, at least in fellowship and caring. . . .

I wish that by some magic I could step to the door and hear it echoing from every house for blocks. *"Suppertime! Come on in, supper's ready!"*

XVI

Elephants on Main Street

In our small town theatrical events were scarce but steady. And there were advantages. With only one thing going on at a time you never had to make choices. That was *it*. And when it was over the spell lasted; you had time to linger over its memory even as you began looking forward to the next.

In winter the pickings were fairly slim. Vaudeville once a month after the movies; the emotion-charged speaking contests at the high school; and a big home-talent musical sponsored almost every year by the Chamber of Commerce. But summer, ah, in summer! You could count on a carnival in summer, usually around the Fourth of July. Every few years a circus came to town (I doubt if we could have stood the excitement more often). And there were two major productions singularly and proudly Storm Lake's: Chautauqua and Sweets Show.

Chautauqua was ours by reason of the gigantic pavilion that had been built on our shores during Chautauqua's heyday. Mother could wax ecstatic about those hal-

cyon days when people came from miles around to pitch
their tents in the park and camp for a week just to attend. "Oh, it was wonderful, I tell you. And we really had
the greats—Billy Sunday, William Jennings Bryan. They
called him the Golden Orator, and he really was. Dr.
Parker was chairman of the committee when I worked
for him, and I helped get out the circulars that year
Bryan came. Dr. Parker introduced me, I got to shake
his hand." Breathlessly—"And you know what he said to
me?"

"Young lady, you're lovely!" we would chorus.

"Well, I don't care, he *did*, and I don't care how many
times I tell it."

Sadly, Chautauqua's popularity was declining. Yet for
several enchanted summers Redpath Vawter continued to
provide a solid week of culture that lured people to that
tall, white, wooden structure whose arches framed the sky.
Its earth floor was sanded, so that your feet crunched,
taking your place among the ranks and ranks of wooden
benches. Strung around all this was a banner of tan canvas so that people who hadn't paid admission couldn't
watch. Some people sat on the thick park grass beyond,
however, and listened.

Dad urged Mother to do this, those years when we
couldn't afford tickets for everybody. She refused; she was
too proud. Even so, you could often hear the orchestras
and the speakers several blocks away, where we lived.
Orators didn't depend on microphones in those days; they
hollered. Besides, the water helped carry the sound; tantalizing shouts and strains of music drifted up, somehow
enhancing the sense of something lonely and sweet, something promising and rather frightening that lay beyond
the confines of our little town.

Mother saw that we got to go to Chautauqua somehow, even if it meant buying one season ticket for the
family and taking turns. One memorable year there was
enough money for season tickets for all three children, and
I'll never forget her pleasure in getting us ready, and
watching us set off, vigorously scrubbed, braided, starched,
and white shoe-polished.

In the morning there was Junior Town—lessons and
games and stunts and singing. My brother was elected
mayor, and on the last day he led a costume parade. In
the afternoon there was usually a lecture or a dramatic
monologue, in the evening a concert or a comedian, and
on the last night a play. Over all this there presided a mas-
ter of ceremonies, always a devastatingly handsome and
genial young man with whom everybody fell hopelessly
in love. Every session was preceded by a little religious
service; then on with the show!

Some kids beat it before the lectures, but I always
sat enrapt. Partly because our father had spent all that
money, partly because Mother would be waiting to hear
every word I could recall. But partly for myself. The fact
that there were people like this, who had traveled so
widely, knew so much, and could speak so eloquently,
was a revelation, profoundly stirring, whetting some awful
ambition to join their sacred ranks.

When Chautauqua was out for the evening and people would begin streaming home past our house, we would
all perch on the front steps and while Dad smoked his
cigar and Mother rocked the baby, we would go into enthusiastic detail about the program. They listened intently,
asking questions, laughing at the right places, sharing.
And at least once during the week the two of them would

get dressed up themselves, and Dad would take Mother to the event of her selection.

Though Chautauqua buffs fought valiantly to save it, its summers were numbered. People were getting too sophisticated with their earphone radios and then their loudspeaker sets; they could hear lectures and concerts at home. Eventually the scene of so much culture stood deserted except for the swallows and pigeons that nested among its rafters, or the kids who played Hide-and-Seek in its dressing rooms or pranced across its stage declaiming to the benches. Benches now stacked in drunken piles, like forlorn and ludicrous monuments to the glory that had been.

But even Chautauqua paled before the thrill of Sweets Show. George D. Sweet had been raised here, until he ran off to marry an actress and founded Sweets Famous Players. And each year, sentimentally, he opened and closed his season by bringing his company "home" for a three-night stand of "Broadway hits." And I doubt if even the people on the Mississippi levees awaiting the arrival of Captain Andy's *Showboat* could have felt more anticipation than we did at the promise of his posters, or the appearance of his tent out behind the Milwaukee depot.

Then you would see them, those gods and goddesses the actors, living so grandly at the Bradford Hotel, riding around town in George D's huge black limousine. A showpiece in itself with its rich gray upholstery, its lace curtains and cut-glass vases that boasted fresh roses daily from Sam Kutz's greenhouse. They were our sole contact with live theater, luring us for a brief span from the shadowy figures that offered such transport on the screen. The fact that they lived and breathed and ate and slept and walked among us for a time enhanced the rapture. We longed to be like them, join them, run away with them from our dreary routine into the Never-Never-Never Land we imagined they inhabited.

For years George D. also had a marching band that would parade down Main Street on opening night, stirring people beyond endurance, so that even if they hadn't planned to, they must follow. And for three bittersweet days the music wagon prowled the sleepy streets pouring out its wistful, wildly appealing tunes. What bliss if you were going, what agony if the prospect was doubtful. In the end Dad often yielded with, "Come on, Mama, get the kids ready—"

"But Sam, we agreed we'd wait till the last performance."

"I know it, doggone it, but we'll figure out a way to go then too." Hopefully. "Maybe G.D. will let us in free."

"Well, don't count on it."

There was always suspense as we clung together in the crowd before the striped marquee. Would it be G.D. himself who parted the canvas and climbed into the box with his cardboard ticket wheel? Or that white-haired grand duchess, Mrs. Sweet, dripping diamonds and Irish blarney, but alert to see that everybody paid? And even when we saw him, that dignified and portly man, usually wearing a pearl-gray hat and smoking a cigar, would he recognize Dad, who claimed to have played with this titan as a boy on the farm?

"Hello there, George, it's me, Sam!" Dad would call out, though Mother nervously tried to shush him. Determinedly he would wriggle and shove his way forward, and if we were lucky the cool, stolid countenance would lift slightly, the great G.D. would nod and beckon, and we would be herded importantly past the ticket taker, with sometimes even a pat on the back and a kindly, "How are you, Sammy?"

Oh, the relief, the power and the glory!

There was the fragrance of trampled grass, the melodic plinking of boards as we clambered to seats in the blue-painted bleachers. Down in front the orchestra was playing, sounding hollow and gay in the vast cup of the tent. Baldy Wetzel, that wizard of the piano, was bouncing up and down on the bench, the keys gone wild, his teeth and his bald dome flashing as he laughed and sang and shouted, sometimes vaulting the bench to kiss a startled lady, or snatch the sticks from the drummer and slash them down the keyboard. His antics competed with the bored voices of the actors calling, "Anybody *else* ovah hear? Anybody *else* ovah heah?" as, already in makeup, they peddled candy along the aisles. Boxes of taffy kisses that might contain a lucky number and win you one of the dazzling prizes displayed onstage: Spanish shawls, fringed lamps, sets of fancy dishes, ukeleles, boudoir dolls, silverware.

Finally all this torment of plunder was hauled away and the actors disappeared backstage. Now you hugged yourself, the better to endure the real suspense, waiting an interminable time for the curtain to rise. When you could bear it no longer the lights would blink, and the curtain with its painting of mountains and waterfalls, its ads for local merchants, would roll up on a setting for sheer enchantment. A romantic comedy, a serious drama, or a mystery. Sometimes a western; but always wholesome, always pure. If these were truly "the best of Broadway, which Mrs. Sweet and I attended all last winter in order to bring you the best possible entertainment," as George D. always claimed in his flat little curtain speeches, they had been rigorously scoured of oaths or anything faintly suggestive. Sweets Show was known in the trade, in fact, as "The Sunday School Show."

We didn't care, we only knew that they made us laugh and cry and dream and long and shiver with delicious fear. *Ghost Train. The Cat and the Canary. Charley's Aunt. Up in Mabel's Room. Abie's Irish Rose. Smilin' Through* . . .

Mrs. Sweet was the undisputed star. When she swept onstage, the entire audience leaped to their feet, unable to contain themselves. At that moment a messenger would dash down the aisle, bearing an armload of red roses to be handed over the footlights. Nightly ritual though this was, she always pretended a vast surprise, wiping away tears as she blew kisses to the frantic crowd. Then, gracefully handing them to an attendant, she would assume her role for the evening. She was especially great in hilarious Irish characters. Running a close second in stardom was her daughter Marjorie, who often played the saucy ingenue.

Between Chautauqua and Sweets Show there was the Fourth of July celebration, often accompanied by a carnival. The hot July day our baby brother was born Dad got rid of us by letting us spend the whole day at the carnival, stuffing ourselves with hot dogs and pop, riding the merry-go-round and trying vainly to win a Kewpie doll. Except for the Kewpies carnivals haven't changed much. Then, as now, there were the barkers, the hootchy-kootchy (girlie) shows, the shooting galleries, the pitch-till-you-win swindles. But the Kewpies—ah, but the Kewpies.

They had taken the country by storm, these plump-bellied, pop-eyed plaster dolls, whose heads swept into a single point. Often elaborately costumed in gilt and crepe

paper, often dressed in nothing but a big satin bow, they
beamed at you from every stand, fat little star-pointed
hands outspread. Proud young swains shot guns or threw
baseballs or whammed an iron hammer to win them for
their girls; couples strolled nonchalantly about, sometimes
carrying a whole flock of Kewpies that would adorn her
piano later (you could almost judge a girl's popularity by
the number of Kewpie dolls and photographs that fought
for space on her piano scarf).

I had been mad for a Kewpie and innocently sure that
I could win one, or my brother could. Only it wasn't that
easy for kids. At the end of the day, though half-drunk
from the orgies of pop and merry-go-round, we trudged
dolefully through the gates, minus a single Kewpie. "Yaaa,
who cares?" my brother tried to console. "We got something better than that to play with when we get home."

I began to hang back, sniveling. "I don't want a baby
brother, I just want a Kewpie!"

At that point a young man came loping after us,
beaming, bright-eyed, not too steady on his feet and with
his straw sailor hat askew. "What's the matter, honey?"

It was the first time a grownup young man had ever
called me honey. I began to bawl in earnest now.

"Aaah, she's just mad because she didn't win a Kewpie," my brother explained in disgust.

"Well, if that's all—why, I been winning Kewpies
all day. C'mon, you too, sister—" and he shepherded all
three of us back to the Hit-the-Kitty stand. The very stand
where we had lost a terrifying amount of money earlier
in the day. Our brother, wise to the ways of the carnival
by now, was skeptical, but we were safe—our money was
all gone. And so we stood there, a goggle-eyed trio, while

this unknown Gallahad wound up, leaned back, and threw. *Thud . . . thud . . . thud!* Incredibly, down went the cats.

"Okay. Now which Kewpie you want, honey?"

I was too dumbfounded to choose; the man behind the counter had to hand me one. Our benefactor turned for another nip from something in his pocket and wound up again. More cats collapsed; my sister was suddenly being presented a Kewpie too. Only she was choosy; she made them take it back and give her the one with the purple skirt and the spangles. I just stood hugging my precious Kewpie, naked except for the huge satin-bow ribbon—I was scared they might change their minds.

"Okay, kids, now go on home, beat it," the guy said suddenly, leaping the counter to join the weatherbeaten man lounging there. Both of them shared the bottle now and grinned at us as we scurried off, too excited to thank them.

We didn't know what to think. I just knew that the fat plaster Kewpie was safe in my arms and its chalky smell was the sweetest smell in the world. I kept sniffing it all the way home.

Every few years a circus came to town. Sells Floto, Yankee Robinson, Clyde Beatty, or lesser ones. Size didn't matter; a circus, any circus, was so awesome, so alien, so exotic it was scarcely to be believed. To think that wild animals would actually be roaring and pacing their cages in our midst, that acrobats and bareback riders would be performing in somebody's pasture! We never felt that a circus belonged to us like Chautauqua or Sweets Show, or even visiting carnivals or the Alta Fair in the fall; a circus was a kind of incredible visitation.

The circus usually arrived in the night, and Dad

would get us up to go down and watch them unload (especially in the years when we couldn't scrape up the money for tickets). Lots of other people had the same idea— there was always a crowd of parents holding sleepy children or leading them by the hand. It was exciting but scary, the hooting whistles, the clanking and squealing as cars were switched about, the waving of lanterns and flashlights, and torches whose tarry smell mingled with the rank citric odor of beasts. Thrillingly, on a siding, was a long line of dark cars where, oblivious to all this, the performers slept.

How could they, in all the commotion? Strange-looking men trudged purposefully about, opening boxcar doors, leading horses down the ramp—and zebras and Shetland ponies, like a line of animated toys. Others drove the great teams of workhorses that were to pull the wagons and the cages. Cages that now waited, ominous and frightening and mostly silent—but now and then a hyena screamed, a lion roared.

"Where are the elephants, Daddy?" a child would ask. "I want to see the elephants." Then everybody would cry out, "Here they come!" Impossibly huge, their gray shapes flowed past in the night, on toward the pasture where some of them would be put to work hauling tent poles. Excitedly we would follow, to watch them moving with amazing grace and precision under the lights. Hammers rang, making a melody of three notes as three roustabouts alternately struck the stakes that held the ropes. Then up it rose, the great white Big Top blossoming, while all about it like some magical garden the smaller tents sprang into being.

The parade was the next day at noon, and this too was almost too impressive. It staggered the senses—the horses

straining at the painted wagons; the band in its gold braid
and plumes, playing from its high, richly ornamented car-
riage; the beautiful, bored-looking girls lurching along on
elephants in gilded trappings; the cages with their pacing
tawny beasts . . . all that Oriental pomp and splendor
moving down Main Street! Past the courthouse and the
post office and the banks, past the barbershop and the two
cafes and the pool hall and the stores. The steam calliope
was last, and its wild plaintive notes were somehow ap-
propriate, eerie, and unsettling.

Sometime during the day came another spectacle, entirely free. The elephants were herded down to the lake
to be watered. Along the street they plodded, toward the
football field and the ice houses, there to wade in, dipping
and lifting their serpentine trunks, sometimes trumpeting
joyfully as they gave themselves showers. We didn't live
far and word traveled fast. "Quick, come quick, elephants
on Main Street, elephants in the lake!" Everything was
dropped, everybody ran, and keeping a respectful distance,
stood open-mouthed. It was like suddenly being catapulted
into a chapter of *Jungle Boy.*

The circus left a kind of glittering ache in the air;
like anything unusual, it aroused our longings. Overnight,
trapezes and tightropes appeared in yards, our bagswings
jolted to newer, more death-defying leaps.

In winter the world of show business passed us by
except for the occasional vaudeville acts at Mike Tracy's
after the movies, and the annual home-talent show di-
rected by a professional from out of town. A musical in
which for several seasons my brother, now old enough,
usually had the lead. It included a chorus of dancing girls.
Aleda Womack and I were wild to be in it. Aleda's mother

sold tickets at the movies so that made Aleda practically a chorus girl herself, we figured. It was she who persuaded the justifiably doubtful director that instead of the simple one-two-three-kick routine she had in mind we all should be ballerinas.

Although none of us had ever set foot in a studio and would have thought "tutu" meant something to do with the evening train, we not only practiced what we fondly believed was ballet, we browbeat our mothers into making our costumes. Despite the fact that it was January and ten below zero, we insisted that our legs and shoulders be bare. Dumbaugh's department store ordered yards of white mosquito netting for the skirts, and for the bodice shiny pink sateen.

Anxious mothers finally gave in, with the stipulation that we be sure Mike Tracy put some extra coal on the furnace for the dress rehearsal as well as the performance. Furthermore, that we promise to get right back into our long winter underwear. There was one holdout, Ruth Mc-Tavish's mother, who was so strict she shuddered at the mere thought of Ruth's dancing, let alone appearing on the stage half nude. When poor Ruth showed up at dress rehearsal her "tutu" drooped almost to her ankles, came to her chin, and had long sleeves. Some people gasped, some laughed, Ruth bawled, and the director had hysterics.

I don't remember how this crisis was resolved. Only that Aleda and I were so enamored of our costumes that after the rehearsal we couldn't bear not to show off. Knowing our mothers would kill us if we didn't, we buttoned ourselves back into the long fleece-lined underwear, and then wore the costumes on top! Our coats bunched out over the fluffy skirts; nor was the effect enhanced by our lumpy, long, black stockings and high-buckle overshoes. But feeling very much the show girls, we left by the stage door and sauntered in and out of stores, sure that we were wowing the town.

The rest of the season people made do with attending the high-school speaking contests and plays. The latter continue; the former, however, have vanished along with a lot of other good things. And it seems to me a pity. Individually it was so exhilarating to be a participant, and collectively it united the community behind its candidates. Also, it was such pure vibrant joyous entertainment.

The art of elocution or "giving readings" was at its height. Young women and often boys would arise at almost every banquet or other occasion to present a monologue. We had several good elocution teachers in town who taught this form, and high schools encouraged it through declamatory contests, in which there were three classifications: oratorical, dramatic, and humorous. First you competed in your own school, then against the others in the county, and finally in the state.

Even the preliminaries were fraught with suspense, and the excitement of the finals packed the high school assembly and overflowed the halls. Stars like Iris Sutton or Katherine Kinne were heavy favorites to win. They delivered their pieces with passion, and not even a high moment at Sweets Show could surpass Iris Sutton's rendition of *The Highwayman*.

> Look for me by moonlight;
>   Watch for me by moonlight;
> I'll come to thee by moonlight, though HELL should
>   bar the way!

Then the sweet terror of her tongue clicking:

Tlot-tlot; tlot-tlot! Had they heard it? The horsehoofs
   ringing clear;
Tlot-tlot, tlot-tlot, in the distance? Were they DEAF
   that they did not hear?

Maybe it was the exposure to all that early Chautauqua, for I went out for "declam" the minute I was eligible
in ninth grade. Nothing so grand as oratorical or dramatic,
but humorous. Mother said she'd coach me. Though nobody suspected it, she had impressive gifts. All I had to do
was to mimic her every gesture and intonation. To everyone's amazement, when the judge's decision was announced, it was our piece that won.

I lay awake all night reliving that first hour of triumph, inspired to press on to others. And did. Later the
school turned me over to professional teachers, but it
was Mother who did the groundwork and it was generally
her original interpretation that was used to best effect.
And oh, the thrill of those big nights in the home high
school, or with a loyal cheering section that had followed
to Cherokee, Le Mars, Fort Dodge. Nights with your
mother looking up with her heart in her eyes and her
hopes in your hands.

An incurable ham, I went out for debate, too, and "ex-
temp" (extemporaneous speaking). And nothing has ever
been of more value than those early experiences of walking onto a platform, trembling, fear-stiff, but suddenly
freed and fired by the sea of expectant faces.

I suppose my children could make a speech if they had
to, but they haven't been put to the test and they couldn't
care less. They just aren't motivated the way I was. They
have never sat enthralled before the magic of Chautauqua,
or had to get up in the night to watch the circus unload

because they couldn't afford admission to the performance. They have color TV and stereo sets; they can attend concerts, see plays traditional or in the round. But I doubt if they have ever experienced the absolute, unadulterated delight we knew in entertainment.

I am glad I was raised in a little town at a time when things didn't happen very often, but when they did they happened grand. I wish, just once, my children could see elephants on Main Street!

XVII

The Secret of
the Christmas Tree

There is no more beautiful celebration of Christmas than in that great city which belongs to all of us, Washington, D.C. Each year a different state ships to the nation's capital its tallest, most magnificent tree. This is erected on the mall, as the crowning feature of the Pageant of Peace. I have stood there with my children awaiting the thrilling moment when, at the touch of the President's hand, that tree springs into fabulous, living light.

We have sat in the National Cathedral, hearing choirs of trained voices present the *Messiah*. We have walked the fairyland of lighted streets. We have gazed into the marvels of animation in store windows, depicting the legends and fantasies of the holiday. On rare occasions when the weather was cold enough, our sons have joined the ice skaters who skim below Lincoln's feet on the famous Reflecting Pool. We have toured the White House decked out in all its festive attire; all the skills of professional artists and decorators combine to achieve perfection in this perfect mansion for this perfect holiday.

But we have always stood longest in the foyer where,

usually, there stands an old-fashioned, ceiling-high, pop-corn- and cookie-trimmed Christmas tree. There are gin-gerbread men too, and quaint and fragile ornaments. There are nuts and fruits and velvet bows such as a mother might have kept in her dresser drawer. There are chains of paper loops like children used to make.

And this, it seems to me, is significant. That in a land of sophistication and plenty, the truest symbol of Christ-mas is, after all, an old-fashioned family kind of tree.

It brings back all the Christmases past that I knew as a little girl. It brings back the winter sports that were their glorious preview: the ice skating, the snow battles, the hopping of bobs. An entire new era of delight was ushered in with the first snowfall, and with the freezing of the lake it became an intense reality.

The lake, that vast rolling body of water in which we had frolicked like savages all summer, became forbidden territory soon after Labor Day. Though it continued to rush shoreward with foaming force, we knew that the days of its might were numbered. Winter was watching from behind the gold, then gradually naked, trees. Soon the water would lie subdued, the first sheets of ice inching out from the shore. Every day some daring boy would test its surface, racing back at the sounds of cracking. But the cold and certain encroachment was taking place; until one day, after severe nights and several false reports, the word would race through town: "The lake's frozen over!" And though parents remained doubtful and issued edicts and warnings, the first few figures began taking tentative swings across its glassy expanse.

"Darn fools," our dad would declare. "You kids aren't setting foot on that ice until we're sure it's safe."

"But it is!" we'd claim. "Old Doc Vanderhoof's been going out every day."

Old Vanderhoof, a retired "horse doctor," was also our local Hans Brinker. Dutch-born, a superb skater. Whenever you saw that tubby figure, arms folded, pipe in his mouth, white whiskers blowing, doing his loops and turns, the parents were assured. The ice was safe.

Our skates had been ready for days. Dug from cellar, barn or attic, sharpened, polished, their worn straps tested, tried on repeatedly. "Now take those things off," Mother scolded, as we clumped or wobbled about. "You'll cut the rug and you'll scar the floor." Each year we inherited bigger ones from older brothers and sisters, and passed ours down. Or you traded with the neighbors. Sometimes the purchase of a new pair was not to be avoided, and, oh, the thrill of those tough, strong, leathery-smelling straps, the brilliance of the blades. Shoe skates were unheard of. It was important, therefore, to have strong thick-soled shoes for the clamps to clutch.

Once, for my birthday in late September, I asked only for my own brand-new ice skates. They seemed unbearably beautiful lying in the box. I'd test their sharpness with a finger, and sometimes, in secret, hold their cold promise against my cheek. The weather seemed unseasonably warm, the wait for their initiation intolerable. Worse, the high-top black shoes with which they were to be worn were getting thin. By the time the ice and the lovely skates were ready, the shoes were shot. It was a lean year, and new ones were out of the question. I had to suffer the ignominy, after all, of some beaten-up old straps across the toes.

We lived only two blocks from the lake. On Saturdays, and most days after school, we hastened down to

The Point, a favorite gathering place. Here a tipsy old green boathouse afforded shelter from the stinging blasts. It was always intensely cold, and though we were lumpy with long underwear and bundled to the eyebrows in layers of sweaters, jackets, leggings, mufflers, mittens, we huddled in its protection, or drew gratefully toward the great crackling fire that older boys often built among the rocks.

Armed with stubby brooms, the boys would have swept the snow aside for a hockey court. And what blithe young gods they seemed as they smacked the little puck with their store-bought or homemade hockey sticks, laughing, yelling, fighting with a fierce and joyous abandon; or often gliding swiftly up to see how the girls were getting along.

There was about them a gallantry and kindness absolutely singular to this contact. At home or at school they might ignore us, tease us, pull our hair or even hit us, but at this gathering upon the ice they became knights in stocking caps and mackinaws. They helped us with our skates; they asked if we were warm enough, and if we weren't they made us go home or sometimes rubbed our hands and feet. They taught the beginners patiently; they steered us about showing us figure eights and how to skate backward, and other fancy tricks. And no matter who it was, even a brother or some dumb neighbor kid, a sense of our own fledgling womanhood was sweetly roused by their attentiveness. While to have one of the true heroes, say a football player or a town lifeguard, kneel at your feet just to tighten a skate was to fall instantly, madly, hopelessly in love.

The boys never suffered us to join their hockey games. And, true Vikings that they were, girls had no place on their iceboats. They fashioned these magical craft them-

selves out of two-by-fours hauled home from the lumber-yard by sled or coaster wagon. These they nailed together crosswise and masted with a piece of canvas, or more likely a mother's bed sheet. The runners and rudders they carved of wood, the runners bladed with strips of metal which were forged and shaped to their purpose by Pat McCabe in his blacksmith shop. We sometimes watched the process, Pat's white teeth flashing in his smoke-black-ened face. The glow of his forge lit up the mysterious re-cesses of his cavern where all manner of interesting ob-jects hung: wagon wheels and horseshoes, pipes and bars and farming tools. There was the smell of hot iron and horses and leather and steam as this skilled and dusky wizard plied his trade.

Perched at front or rear of the boats, or lying flat, the boys steered these fleet ships into vast blue gleaming dis-tances of the lake where only a foolhardy skater dared venture. (There were air holes; every now and then the town was shaken by some skater's shooting into such a hole and being trapped beneath the ice. This was our parents' greatest concern.) But the ice boaters were charmed beings, winged by the wind, flying safe and free.

Boys also fought pitched battles behind their snow forts, and here the girls were allowed, if only in the capacity of providing ammunition. Our job was to make the snowballs, and we gloated over our growing stock, much as our mothers proudly counted their canning. A good snowball maker was much in demand. I always envied Gert Beatty who was first to be chosen when she trudged out. She fashioned round, firm snowballs with the same methodical skill that she turned out loaves of bread for her mother, or a firm, creamy platter of fudge. Hers put my leaky, lopsided snowballs to shame. An even higher honor was accorded Kac Ford, a girl who knew more about football than most boys, and had such a terrific pitching arm she was not only allowed on the team, she sometimes led the charge.

Yet for sheer exhilarating delight nothing could equal hitching bobsled rides. With the onset of winter, cars were hoisted onto blocks to protect the tires, and stored away. There were simply no facilities for sweeping the snow-muffled streets. Townspeople walked (or waded) to their destination; country people traveled by bob. Saturday was the big trading day in town, and consequently the best day for hopping bobs. Farmers approaching Storm Lake by almost any road were met by a swarm of kids, most of them pulling sleds. If you didn't have a sled you hopped on the long wooden runner and hung onto the wagon box. With a sled you looped its rope over a bolt at the back or through a brace at its side.

A good-natured farmer usually "Whoa-ed" his team to a halt so that you could get attached, or he at least slowed down. A mean one, spying the eager contingent, would whip his horses on faster. It was fun to run madly after him, trying to catch him anyway. It added to the

thrill. Hooking a ride with someone who didn't even sus-
pect you were there was especially exciting, dangerous as
it was. He might make a sudden turn or stop and throw
you off.

Parents were always issuing futile edicts against the
hopping of bobs. Yet they, too, remembered the thrill of
lying belly-flat upon a sled that went whistling and bouncing across the crusty and glittering ground—here bumpy,
here glass-smooth, here stained mustard-yellow, here grayly
tramped, here purest shining white . . . while up front
there was the steady plocking rhythm of the horses' hooves,
the jingle of harness, the creak and rattle of the wagon box,
while sometimes wisps of straw flew back like pinfeathers
from angel wings.

Clutching the wooden rudders of our sleds, we steered,
avoiding the deeper ruts; and rounding a corner, trying
not to swing too far to the side. You could lose your grip,

skid off, hit a curb, a lamppost, or be hurled into the path of an oncoming team. Thus the perils, tempering our pleasure, yet enhancing it.

Bobsleds were great to ride in, too, out to Grandpa Holmes' or an uncle's, snuggled down on the tickling straw. We made tents of the scratchy, raw-smelling horse blankets, and burrowed down like groundhogs, cozy and squirming, with sometimes a heated soapstone or a hot, carpet-wrapped brick at our feet. We played pioneer—we were crouched in a covered wagon, and the amiable small-town sounds beyond or the whistling wind of the open country were the threatening howls of wolves or Indians.

Even Santa Claus came by bobsled. A couple of weeks before Christmas his impending arrival was proclaimed by the businessmen. Everybody gathered downtown, kids shoving and falling off the curbs in frantic anticipation. Then came the sweet, familiar jangling of his sleighbells, and there was the old boy himself, waving a mittened paw and tossing out bags of candy while some assistant drove the team.

A free show at the movie followed. "To get us kids out of the way so our folks can buy our presents," smart-alecky older ones claimed. We were doubtful and stricken. But we'd just seen him. "Aaah, that was just ole Matt McDermott dressed up," hooted the heretics sitting behind. And they jiggled the musty velour seat. "We peeked through the courthouse window and seen him stuffing a pillow down his pants!" It was too funny, and too awful to believe. Yet it didn't really matter. Sucking blissfully on the hard painted candies, watching Tom Mix or Harold Lloyd, we were content in the awareness of some loving adult conspiracy on our behalf.

The fantasy of Santa Claus seemed not in the least at

odds with the mail-order catalogs, over which we crouched, making long, drunken lists which must be whittled down to plausible proportions. Nor with the noisy bedlam of shopping in our little stores. Nor with the hum of Mother's sewing machine at night. Over and over we'd ask, "What for?" if only to hear the beloved reply: "What fur? Cat fur to make kitten britches!" Pressed, she might admit that she was helping Santa's elves. "He's not going to be able to do as much as he'd like to this year." Then, among the few new toys of Christmas morning we would find bean bags, doll clothes, little cloth purses for Sunday School.

The old pine chest in the storeroom held all sorts of oddments from which she drew: scraps of flannel left over from diapers, velvet and gingham, quilt blocks, buttons, embroidery cotton. Here she hid both her handiwork and her purchases; and it was understood by all that no one looked in the box. The most miserable Christmas I ever had was the year I yielded to temptation and found what I most desperately wanted, a real, working Ouija board.

Mother exchanged gifts with a number of chums who lived elsewhere—Aunt Tressa, Aunt Anna, Aunt Mabel, as we called them. She worked openly on their presents, tatting or crocheting doilies and edgings, her shuttle dipping like a little fat bird, the dainty beak of her crochet hook plucking and pulling and picking—almost tasting the threads. She wrapped her efforts in white tissue paper, thin as new snow, and bound them with silver cords. And those rectangles of white and silver seemed in their loveliness to be jeweled blocks for the palace of the Ice Princess.

By now she would have brought forth the family decorations—rough ropes of red and green to loop above the lace curtains and garland the living room. And several paper bells, which lay flat until unfolded, when lo! they

bloomed fat and full to hang in doorways and dance in the heat of the hardcoal stove. For us, as for most people, this was all. And while the churches boasted Christmas trees, they were almost unknown in private homes when I was very small.

I shall never forget our first one. Two gentle maiden ladies who lived next door called Mother over one day; and when she returned she was excitedly bearing an enormous box. Desperate for its secret, we plagued her until she yielded at least initials: C.T.D. We spent almost as much time trying to guess their meaning as learning our pieces for the Christmas Eve program at church.

This program, at first mostly songs and recitations, later a pageant, was as much a part of Christmas as hanging up your stocking. We practiced religiously, and if possible got a new dress. Snow squeaked underfoot and sparkled under the streetlights as the family walked to the church. Grandpa Griffith, who was janitor, always built a big fire early. The church was warm and spicy with the scent of the tall fir tree beside the stage. Standing over the hot-air register, we admired the way our skirts ballooned.

Sunday School teachers frantically began assembling angels in their proper rows. Shadows moved behind white sheets hung up for curtains. Garbed in bathrobes and turbaned in towels, your father and other men became strangers saying, "Let us go now even unto Bethlehem and see this thing which has come to pass . . ." And the click and swish of the sheets being pulled—and at last the revelation: For there stood Joseph beside a manger with real straw! And Mary cradling a baby—sometimes a big doll, but once a real baby! The minister's new baby! You could hear it crowing and glimpse a flailing hand. It lived! And for a breathless, rapturous moment the living, breathing Christ Child was right there in your midst.

After the pageant there was an anxious, squirming hush in which you knew something else magical was about to happen. A jangling of sleigh bells heightened the suspense as the superintendent asked, "What's that? Do I hear somebody?" And the wild and frenzied screaming as he appeared, so big and jolly he sometimes almost knocked over the red cardboard fireplace climbing out—"Santa, Santa Claus!"

As you grew older he began to look familiar—like Mr. Samsel or Simon Thomas, but no matter—when he patted your head or handed you a bag of hard candies he became the droll elf of the eternal fairy tale of North Pole and Make-Believe.

And the Ladies Aid served cookies and coffee, and parents visited, and children, mad with anticipation, begged to go home lest he miss their house . . . And at last you all poured out onto the steps that had been paved with ground diamonds.

"Good night, Merry Christmas, come to see us!" voices called as families set off along the cold sparkling streets. The snow had usually stopped by now. The night was still and clear. All the stars glittered. But there was always one bigger and brighter than the rest. A great gem that seemed to stand still as if to mark the mystery. And you gazed at it in wonder all the way home.

There you scurried for bed and lay hugging yourself, listening to the sweet lullaby of Christmas Eve—parental voices murmuring, the rattle of paper, the tinkle and squeak of treasures unguessed.

Awake before daylight, we found Mother already in the room to restrain us. "Wait!" she said. Something strange was going on. Then when a voice called, "Ready, Rose," she led us forth—into fairyland. Or so it seemed. For there in the living room bloomed a miracle: a Christmas tree! Its candles twinkled and fluttered as if hosts of butterflies and birds had alighted on its branches. From its arms gleamed dozens of fragile beads and baubles and ornaments. We stared at it, eyes shining, too dazzled to speak.

And now we knew the secret of the box, C.T.D. "Christmas Tree Decorations," Mother laughed. "The

Misses Spicer had them as young ladies in Europe and want our family to have them now."

This lovely gift became the basis for all the trees that followed. We augmented it with strings of popcorn, paper chains, gilded walnuts, and later, when they were plentiful, cranberries. The exquisite fragrance (and hazard) of the tallow candles was replaced by electric bulbs, while tinsel and icicles and fine new ornaments almost crowded out those exquisite early ones. But no tree, however splendid, will be as beautiful as that first one. And no gifts, however expensive or plentiful, can surpass the joy of those precious few we found under it that day . .

Today Santa travels by jet or helicopter instead of bobsled or sleigh. We hear a lot about the commercial Christmas, the cocktail party instead of church on Christmas Eve. But we also have a Pageant of Peace in our nation's capital, based on the message of the Christ Child, and the eyes of the world are turned upon it as our President launches that pageant with the lighting of the national Christmas tree. While in the White House (which is your house, too, and mine) there stands a symbol of the invincible American family, an old-fashioned tree.

Thank goodness, despite all other changes, this one thing remains. It is the secret of our freedom and our greatness. It is the true secret of America, its magic and its stability. It is the secret of the Christmas tree.

EPILOGUE

"Come Home"

What is this strange compulsion to go home again? The place you were so anxious to leave, yet can never leave altogether. Too much of you is rooted there. You thought that you were tearing yourself free, bloodily by the roots, yet fragments always remain tenaciously. They are stronger than you think. They tug at you when you go back, they tease and torment you. They people the street with ghosts, one of them yourself. "This is where you began, where you belong. Come back!" they seem to call.

Yet as Thomas Wolfe said, "You can't go home again." The change is almost too much to bear. And yet the sameness, the sweet tantalizing sameness . . .

When I was home the spring before Mother died we all piled into the car one night after supper and went for a ride. It was sunset, one of those dazzling, burning sunsets that turn the lake to molten gold and stirred me so as a girl. The same docks jutted, the same gulls wheeled, the same droves of little black mudhens were riding, plunging, riding their crests as the same tireless waves foamed in. The lake, mysterious old gray-green friend, was rolling in as it has for generations. Grandpa Griffith was chased across it by the wolves one winter. Grandpa and Grandma fished here, Mother and Dad courted in its shady parks. And so did we. Every walk and bench and statue is a silent shout of memories.

But change has disturbed its shores. Manawa Beach, where we used to hike and drink the cold spring water, is now suburbia. Even the farms whose pastures went down to the water have been broken up for handsome new homes. Showplaces all, straight out of magazines. My brother pointed them out: "The Schallers built that place. Next door is Dick Richardson. That's Zene White's—" On and on. He and his wife know them all, and the names they recite are often familiar but just as often strange. "The Hershbergers? Oh, he's the new coach at Buena Vista college. The Dyvads built that one—Harry's on the city council now." My brother and his wife never left our little town, and its occupants and alterations are as familiar to them as the doings of their own family.

There are other changes more staggering. Gone is Curt Bethard's huge old weather-scarred boathouse where we learned to swim and hung around all summer, savage-brown, always in love, waiting for life to happen. Now a cement hole in the ground attracts the kids instead. You hear them laughing and shouting, catch a whiff of chlorine from the pool, and feel a kind of affront for the fishy old lake still bashing bravely in. (What's the matter with kids today? We were never daunted by its mighty muscles, we loved its cold embrace. Even on the roughest days or when it was paint-green we went in!)

But branching up from the parks in all directions are

many of the selfsame houses on the selfsame streets. There
is solace in this, and a curious pain. How can they be
here exactly as when you passed them on your way to
school or played in them as children? Like the lake, they
seem timeless, rooted in sameness forever, totally unaware
that you have left and spent a lifetime elsewhere. And it
seems that if only you would get out and go to them, you
too would be the same. Back someplace in time again,
safe with vigorous young parents who loved you, and your
heart was not yet broken.

As we drove idly up and down it became a senti-
mental journey, for we began to call out the names of the
people who once lived in these houses. "Redenbaughs were
on the corner, the Beattys next door, then the Pattees—
she was always so pretty—"

"Then the Crowleys," another voice would say, "and
across the street the Sheffields. Remember how Gordon
Sheffield used to hang around wanting to play with us
older kids?" It became a kind of contest to see who could
remember first. Up and down the streets we cruised, piec-
ing the past together through these names. Sometimes
arguing, "No, the Roops *didn't* live there, it was the Ring-
enbergs. I oughta know, it's where I broke my arm when
their bagswing broke and Mr. Ringenberg bawled me out
because he'd have to buy a new rope!"

Laughter, a merry uniting of memories along with
that dull ache . . . Our pilgrimage draws us even farther
into the past. There stands the house where my brother
was born. There the house where my parents were married. There even the small white cottage behind a hedge
"where Dad and I met," Mother says. "At a church party.
I'd come with another boy, but he walked me home."

Incredible! It mustn't be there any more in its prim white dignity, looking as it must have looked that night. For now, impossibly, one parent is gone and the other is old and must soon be going. "Come back!" the mute houses are crying. "Nothing is different, nothing is changed. Come home." . . .

A few months later the phone rang: it was the call I'd been expecting, and it said, "Come home."

A hometown puts its arms around you when a parent dies. It gathers you to itself like a child. It feeds and comforts you. People surround you, warm living people, and they too say with their food and flowers and their eyes: "Stay. Oh, don't go away again, stay home."

Sometimes they even say it aloud.

Church, the Sunday after the funeral . . . and she wasn't in her usual pew. She wasn't leading the dwindling Bereans (the "old people's class") downstairs clutching their worn Bibles. Mother played the organ for years when we were little; and she taught from the Beginners through Teens, Young Marrieds and finally these chipper but faltering few. "Where do they go when they graduate from your class now?" someone once asked her, and she laughed, "To heaven, I hope!" There were so few of them left to gather in that little classroom with its nostalgic smell of all church basements—coffee, hymnals, crayolas. And they looked so lost without her.

But it was Dick, a boy I grew up with, who put it into words after the sermon: "Come back, Marj. We need you. This is where you belong."

I felt strangled. There had been nothing for me here in years; why now? Why this strange compulsion now?

For the temptation, however absurd, was intense, and the rejection violent.

"You don't understand. I couldn't." . . .

We spent days breaking up her home. Boxing up memories, keepsakes, and photographs that we'd probably never look at again but couldn't bear to part with. Dividing things, giving things away, cleaning. I walked across the backyard to throw out some trash. The arbor needed painting but still supported the torrent of red roses Dad had set out years ago and took such pride in. They climbed all over the garage and trailed the ground, greedy with life. They were almost too fragrant in the hot sun, their petals spilling. Great trees still arched the yard as if still waiting for family picnics on the grass, great gatherings of the clan. Mother's bag of clothespins was still hanging on the line.

My sister came out and we maundered about the place, remembering. And I said, "Why is man the only creature to experience this awful tie with his past? Memory is both a blessing and a curse, it hurts to recall the days which are over."

"That's because we remember only the good things about them. Looking back it always seems so much better." Then she said, "But man needs memory. Without memory there wouldn't be any painters or writers—no doctors to help us, no engineers, no architects. Memory is what enables man to survive and progress."

And this is true, but it's more than that. Man is the only creature whose emotions are entangled with his memory. And the anguish of memory is what we probably must pay for its pleasures, or whatever progress we gain from it. Bitter or sweet, we don't want any part of life to be really over; it should always be available, if only through people who have shared it. When they go they take a part of you with them. Even when something goes that has been a part of your life story—even that old wooden boathouse.

But the roots remain. The roots that will forever keep calling you back, begging, *"Come home!"*